# Dr. Roy E.
# Musings & Contemplations
# of the Sacred Scripture

**Thoughts for the Mystic (*spiritual seeker*)
to Contemplate**

*My teachings are not my own; they come from the One who sent me.*

### BOOK 1

In my book, you will find 150 of my Musings and
Contemplations to meditate on yourself.

As of March 2023, Roy has published 30 books of his own, and many for other people. Got to www.lulu.com/spotlight/royrichmon.com

More Books published by Author: Dr. Roy E. Richmond
**Paperback and eBooks are available.
@ https://www.lulu.com/spotlight/royrichmond
A few are also available
@ https://tinyurl.com/RERAmazonBooks

Dr. Roy E. Richmond's Musings & Contemplations of the Sacred Scripture – Book 1

Unveiling Apostle Paul's Epistles to Rome and for us. Volumes 6-8, with more to come. This is part of the Spiritual Code and Symbolism of the Living Word series.

The Revelation of the Apostle, taught to him by Jesus and the Essenes. Five volumes of the Spiritual Code and Symbolism of the Living Word series – volumes 1-5.

What's in a Name – Volumes 1 & 2. Authored by Dr. Kay Fairchild and Dr. Roy E. Richmond

The Essays of Dr. Roy E. Richmond, from the Masters of Arts Biblical Studies.

The Essays of Dr. Roy E. Richmond, from the Masters of Arts Biblical Theology.

The Essays of Dr. Roy E. Richmond, from the Masters of Arts Biblical Counseling.

Roy E. Richmond Tree of Life Bible Translations – Volume 1.

The Mystical (Spiritual) View of the book of Romans, fully translated.

The Wisdom of the Single Eye

The Wisdom of Spiritually Minded Counsel

You are the True Light of the World

How Esther Became a Star

No Penal Substitution, Volume 1, 2 & 3 Co-Authored by Dr. Kay Fairchild & Dr. Roy E. Richmond

Living Out of Your Spiritual Resources, Volume 1 & 2 Co-Authored by Dr. Roy E. Richmond & Dr. Kay Fairchild – order @ this link - https://py.pl/1t4Yav
Both books are for $20, including priority shipping in the USA only.

The Apostle Paul's letters to the Community of Believers at Galatia and Ephesus.
RERichmond Tree of Life Bible Translation - Paraphrased and Allegorically Explained

# Dr. Roy E. Richmond's Musings & Contemplations of the Sacred Scripture

DrRoyERicmond@cox.net for information.

625 SW 158th Terrace

Oklahoma City, OK 73170

405-204-0713 Central Time USA

**Book One**

Copyright 2023 RERichmond Publishing

ISBN #978-1-312-7351-8

The writings in this book are from over 35 years of studying Scripture, many books, and many resources from the writings of the Ancients. For my biblical translations, I use PC Bible Soft – Strongs Interlinear. I only use the meanings of the Hebrew and Greek words; I do not use what Mr. Strongs wrote after the actual definition.

I take no credit for being the originator of anything I teach. Father is the Source of all knowledge and wisdom; I depend on Father's Voice within my thoughts, for all I write, and the many resources of ancient writers. You have my permission to teach from this book; but please do not reprint this document in any format – paperback book or an eBook; the book is copyrighted.

# Book of Life

**We are the Book of Life**; therefore, we must go within to learn the truth of the Word so that the Truth will be evident in what we write, teach and share with others.

Although the Sacred Scriptures are mostly universally considered the printed Bible only, the accurate Scriptures are the Book of Life within our Divine Mind, flowing to our conscious awareness. The written Word is as a clue to a more vital part of the Scriptures than appears since they have both a literal and a spiritual significance.

The true meaning of the Bible is a Divine "Book of Life" rather than merely a history of people, and it bears "witness unto the word of God (Acts 14:3). The word (*logos*) spiritually means the living, creative spiritual law-giving, and revealing activity of truth.

When we understand this power of the living, creative spiritual law-giving, and revealing activity of truth (*Logos*), we have the key to the imperishability of sacred writings. According to tradition, all the writings of the Hebrew Bible were destroyed; but they were restored by Esdras, who remembered in his awareness and rewrote them. Modern discoveries in the realm of understanding explain in a measure this spiritual statement. We know now that every word that man utters makes an imprint in the spiritual atmosphere. Where there is the consciousness of God-life in the Divine Mind influenced consciousness awareness of the teacher/speaker, their words become living identities preserved throughout the ages. Anyone who develops sufficient spiritual power (*understanding*) may enter this Book of Life within the Divine Mind and spiritually read and teach from its pages.

I pray that what I study, write, and teach from the Book of Life within me, brings you, the reader, a greater understanding of the living, creative spiritual law-giving, and revealing activity of Truth.

# ABOUT THE AUTHOR

Roy Richmond is the President and founder of Tree of Fellowship and Tree of Life Ministries International, Inc. He ministers worldwide through the World Wide Web, Facebook, and YouTube and serves as a Professor at GlobalGraceSemiary.org. Roy has earned a Doctorate Degree in Theology, Master of Arts Theology, Master of Arts Biblical Studies, and Master of Arts Biblical Counseling. He has traveled abroad and across the United States, ministering with a "clear sounding" Word. Father has equipped Dr. Roy as a Scribe to the nations. Scribes represent the thoughts that come to us from Father; Father inspires us from within. The Logos he teaches is the creative spiritual law-giving and revealing activity of the inspired Word of Father. When Spirit speaks, no person can be quoted as authority--the Truth itself is authority, and it bows to no individual interpreter. Roy's web page is filled with many books that are offered for those who hunger and thirst after the Truths Jesus revealed, which is commonly titled "The Gospel." He is an Apostle/Mentor to many fellowships of the Community of Believers. The mandate and anointing on Pastor Roy's life is to eat the fat, drink the sweet, and send portions unto them for whom nothing is prepared. (Neh. 8:10).

As you read my books, please be aware when I translate Scripture from Hebrew and Greek, I only pay attention to the meaning of the words I search for; I do not pay attention to what Mr. Strong wrote afterward. No matter what the intention, Mr. Strong and other authors of Interlinear books added their doctrinal beliefs to the definition of the words. The Apostle Paul wrote to Timothy, and in his letter, he wrote, "All scripture given by inspiration of Father, is profitable for doctrine..." The translators add "is," as "in All Scripture is given..." Therefore, we know that all the words in the written Word is not of Father, but many statements come from the false perceptions of the writer and wrong translations.

Unless otherwise identified, Scripture quotations are from the RERichmond Tree of Life Bible Translations, King James, Amplified Version, and the Message Translation. The Greek and Hebrew references are from Biblesoft's New Exhaustive Strong's Numbers and Concordance with Expanded Greek-Hebrew Dictionary: copyright (c) 1994, Biblesoft and International Bible Translators.

# PREFACE

**To Pastors, Teachers, and Mystics who search the spiritual meaning of Scripture (*the Living Word*), and to all the family of this planet who will read the words of this book:**

Like the Apostle Paul, I am "fighting the good fight "by penning and teaching several books and thousands of pages of unpublished writings. These writings are based on biblical teachings inspired by the Divine Mind within. I have not finished my "fight" of faith yet. I continue to translate Scripture, study, teach and write. I have placed my confidence in our Father, and Father has guided me along this path. At the beginning of my studies and writings in 1988, I was apprehended by an insatiable desire to study Scripture. I was privileged to study under several wonderful pastors and teachers. The first was John Courson of Jacksonville, Oregon, whom I had never met. I transcribed all of his teachings from 1988 to 1996. Another of my mentors was the late Gary Garner of Danville, AR. I also transcribed the majority of his teachings from 1996 to 2012. Then Father spoke to my thoughts and said, "You can quit transcribing from others' teachings; I will give you what to teach and write."

Through Gary Garner, I then met John Cahill of Lancaster, SC. I learned much from brother Garner and John Cahill. Through these three men, my understanding opened to the "Written" Word. I gleaned from them more than I ever learned from my childhood church of 38 years or the two Bible seminaries I attended. I am forever thankful for their impact on my walk of faith.

As remarkable to me (*and others*) as their teachings were, they were all based on the false doctrine of Penal Substitutionary Atonement. This wrong theory states: "Someone had to die and suffer for those who deserved to die and be punished."

According to this doctrine, all people were included in needing a substitute, "world without end." Hugo Grotius introduced the doctrine of Penal Substitutionary Atonement in the 17th century. It states that Jesus suffered for humanity so God could forgive humans without punishment while maintaining divine justice. Early Christian notions of the person and the sacrificial role of Jesus in (supposed) human salvation were further elaborated by the Church Fathers, medieval writers, and modern scholars in various other atonement theories. These theories include the ransom theory, the Christus Victor theory, the recapitulation theory, the satisfaction theory, and the penal substitution theory. Some will say,

"Then why do our bibles teach this theory or doctrine of Penal Substitution?" My answer is: the translators of the written Word, and those who controlled them, translated the Scripture from Latin to German and then to English. They attempted to "dumb us down" and make us think that we were "less than Father," "less than Jesus," or "less than Mary." They also wanted us to believe these things: 1) in a Trinity that is much higher than us, 2) that we can never really know Father, or 3) or be One with Father. I call what they did "The Great Lie." I aim to uncover what religiosity has placed over the Apostle Paul's revelation. Then all will "clearly" see what Father Jesus and the Essenes, the mystical sect of the Jewish religion, taught Paul for three years in the desert. Father has revealed, during my studies, all of this to me, which I now write.

While studying the doctrine of Penal Substitutionary Atonement, I knew Father as "God." It was challenging to believe, but I did think that Father needed appeasement, and Mankind needed to be saved and "stop sinning." These are just the symptoms of the Only sin, which is believing the mistaken identity being enforced by religiosity. The first Race of Mankind listened to teachers (trees) of the knowledge of good and evil. I also partook in those teachers from my early youth until 2012.

Now, after studying with Dr. Kay Fairchild for many years and our writing five books together (Living out of our Spiritual Resources, volumes 1 & 2, and No Penal Substitution, volumes 1, 2 & 3), I no longer know our Creator as "God," but as Father, Source, Holy Breath and Papa. The cool thing is that Father eternally knows us all as Son or Daughter, in the perfect likeness and ONE.

Since awakening to a greater understanding of Spiritual Truth, I now study as a Mystic. A mystic seeks the spiritual Truth of the Living Word. I have often considered correcting the false teaching and translations of the Penal Substitutionary Atonement theory. These teachings are often called "The Pauline Revelation" and "The Apostle Paul's Seven Pillars of Truth." To do this would be a tremendous endeavor for anyone. When I thought about correcting these misconceptions and wrong translations of the Revelation Apostle Paul learned, I thought, "This would be too hard of a task." I decided to keep writing and teaching my other books. After all, Kay Fairchild and I wrote three books titled "No Penal Substitution," which would explain it enough. Studying and writing those three books took me over three years, plus all the time Dr. Kay took to research and teach the subject herself.

But then again, I have learned when I experience a prod to write on a biblical subject; it is a mandate from Father. I have found that the drive will not stop until I document what has been placed on my awareness.

Like the Apostle Paul, I did not learn what I know from "Man whose breath is in his nostrils." I no longer learn or listen to people whose only knowledge of the Word comes from their 5-sense understanding. A serious student of the Living Word must seek out those who are spiritually mindful – mystics. When you read Paul in Scripture, where he wrote, "What I've learned, I learned from no man," the word Man is Anthropos, meaning human-minded, as opposed to spiritual mindfulness. He did not seek approval from the disciples because they had not yet been apprehended by what Jesus sought to teach them. Jesus said, "You cannot or will not bear (understand) the things I have taught you." He also told them Father would send many more Comforter Messengers, teachers, and explainers of the Truth of the Living Word. The Apostle Paul and then John were two of these comforter messengers. Many others have come to help us after Jesus. Many more will come in the future. I am not ashamed to say, "I am one." I continue to learn, eat the fat, and drink the sweet. Then send portions (mana) to them for whom nothing is prepared by their teachers, for every day is holy to our Father. Do not be sorry for what you have not learned. Be glad in what you are learning now; it will produce great joy and strengthen you.

I have confidence in my view of Father and the understanding of the Living Word being corrected by my Holy Breath. So, hang on, and get ready to learn of the Living Word, as revealed to the Apostle Paul and then clearly taught by him in all his Epistles.

I pray for the blessings of seeing and hearing what the Holy Breath of our Father within has to reveal as you read the following Musings and Contemplations of the Sacred Scripture. I will write and publish a second volume soon.

## What is Man?

Allegoriaclally, Adam' is the first movement of awareness in its contact with Divine life and substance (*Divine Mind/Father*). Adam' also represents the universal Man, or the whole race of Man represented in an individual-man idea. Eve is the feminine aspect of universal Man, outwardly manifest: "Male and Female created HE them, to reproduce HIMSELF."

If the ego, or will, which is in Man, has faithfully adhered to Divine wisdom and carried out in its work the plans that are idealized in Wisdom, it has created a harmonious consciousness. Adam' in the Garden of Eden is symbolical of that consciousness.

Adam' in his original creation was in spiritual illumination. Holy Breath Breathed into them continually the necessary inspiration and knowledge to give superior understanding. But they began eating, or appropriating, ideas of two powers; God and not God, or good and bad, have and have not. As the allegory relates, the result was that they fell away, in their awareness, from spiritual life and all that it involved in contact with Father.

Man is Holy Breath, absolute and unconditioned, but Man forms a consciousness into which he breathes the Breath of life; this, in its perfect expression, is the Son of Man, an expression of the Divine idea of Father. This Adam' is all of what we term Soul, which embodies intellect and body. We are continually at work with our Soul; we can breathe the Breath of Life into our understanding, inspiring ourselves with the idea of Life in all Its unlimited fullness. We can lift our conscious awareness by infusing these magnificent ideas in no other way.

Heaven – what is heaven?

Heaven is the Christ consciousness, the realm of the Divine Mind, a state of consciousness in harmony with the thoughts of the Father. Heaven is everywhere present, and it is the arranged, lawful adjustment of Father's kingdom in Man's Divine Mind, Awareness, and Affairs of life.

Jesus, of all those claiming intimate acquaintance with spiritual things, gave heaven a definite location. "The kingdom of God is within you" (Luke 17:21). Heaven is the consciousness of Truth formulated and established for eternity; it's infinite. Heaven is within every one of us; a place, a conscious sphere of mind, having all the attraction described or imagined as belonging to heaven. But this kingdom within is not material; it is spiritual; IT is knowing you are right-wise with Father and the eternal peace, perfection, and joy that comes from knowing you are One with Father. Within our Divine Mind, eternally new ideas manifest on the earth. Isaiah said, "The whole earth is full of God's glory." Isaiah also said, "The whole world is at rest and is quiet: they break forth into singing. Glory is to magnify with praise (telling the story) and enhance with spiritual splendor, to adorn. Glorification is the highest spiritual state of consciousness within reach of Man. We are Father's glory; we must only become aware of and embrace this fact. Isaiah saw with his single eye the truth of all Mankind being the glory of Father and at perfect rest, being calm and quiet with Father.

Spiritually, "jewels of silver and jewels of gold" represent wisdom and love in an external sense. This means we are to affirm all wisdom and all love; even in their most external manifestations, they are spiritual. This puts Spirit (*Breath*) in control both within and without and does away with the external ego – me, myself, and I. When the flood of wisdom, knowledge, and understanding (*Light*) from our Divine Mind is let in through our declaration of the One wisdom, One understanding, One knowledge (*Omniscience*), and One love, this I (*ego*) of every liable to die (*mortal*) state of consciousness is slain, and not one person lives AS dead to their contact with Father. Paul wrote, "It is no longer "I" (me, myself and I).... But the Life I know live is in contact with my Divine Mind, with IT's creative spiritual law giving and revealing activity. (paraphrased by me)

What is abundance? Abundance is spiritual, not material. Madonna sang the song "I'm a material girl." At one time or another, most people could sing the same theme of themselves. Our true Abundance is the ideas in the consciousness of the omnipresent supply and support of the One Divine Mind within. It is an invisible substance with an infinite capacity for expansion when held in one's awareness, affirmed, and consistently articulated in one's thoughts. The invisible substance and supply cannot be explained to material-minded persons, for the substance and supply of spirit must be recognized by the spiritually aware. Jesus said, "All

From birth to death, we are trained to fear, look for, and expect bad in the form of disease. We are taught to expect our bodies to fail to maintain health and vigor as we grow older. We are trained to see the bad in other people, perhaps who might try to steal from us or take advantage of us for their gain. We are plagued by the promises of the leaders of the systems of the cosmos, whom we have wrongly depended upon, who have now disappointed us, deceived us, and hindered us in many ways. We are afraid of accidents, weather, seasonal changes, plants, trees, flowers, animals, and insects. We never have enough and are always in fear of losing what meager portions we do have. We are looking at the experience that should be filled with life from the eyes of death. This is the veil that needs to be removed from man's thinking, which is what the Apostle Paul called "The sin in our members" (subconscious).

The things we perceive as lack, disease, and poverty are not the enemy; the enemy is what we were taught and trained to believe and accept in our subconscious, which perceives evil. The present human-minded awareness, which is

Man's breath that is in his nostrils (*sensory understanding thinking*) is the only thing from which needs to be delivered. Anyone can be delivered if they enter Father's perfect rest, relax and receive the engrafted creative spiritual law giving and revealing activity of Father with meekness.

When our subconscious is cleansed of all that is not Truth, the light of the Glory of the One Life appears, and all things appear different. Jesus repeated time and time, "Don't judge." Your judgment is only coming from what you have learned and perceived with the eyes of your subconscious. You are seeing the manifestation of what you have wrongly believed. You have heard the saying, "Seeing is believing." I say, "believing is seeing."

A definition of the human-mindful subconscious is an imagery of popular belief, floating with the popular current of mortal thought, without questioning the reliability of its conclusions. So, we do what others do, believe what others believe and say what others say; therefore we experience what others experience.

When we enter the conscious space of Breath, when we allow Holy Breath to live ITs Life as us, and when we allow our true nature to be our nature, all the rules are automatically fulfilled just by loving and being loved. It is then that we live Life naturally, with no effort. Our subconscious is cleansed of all that hinders us, and our Divine Mind (Father) drives our conscious awareness (thought, intellect, and emotions).

We need a conscious awakening to the inner light (*wisdom, knowledge, and understanding*) of our being, awakening by Man to their true self, to his Divine Sonship. The result is a treasuring, unifying, gathering together of this awakening consciousness by our Divine Mind, and its growth, further unfoldment, to the end that the individual may be wholly lifted out of limited, carnal thought into the fullness of the one Mind

This picture of creation, as God created it and sees it, is in direct contrast to the story we have been taught and have

lived under for over 6,000 painful years. It is time that we let go of that story. We must no longer see ourselves either as worthy or unworthy. The whole question of worthiness is not an issue at all. We are just what we are: the object of Divine Love and the expression of Divine Love. Father described Himself to Moses as "I Exist that I Exist." We are the expression of the One Eternal Life. We are one with all that IS. We must let go of the version of a God whose favor we need to earn. We must let go of a remote place called heaven, which we also need to earn the right to enter. The kingdom of heaven is, and always has been, within us. We must feel and express love and know and realize that we are loved.

**Kingdom of heaven:** *Being right-wise with Father, and the peace, perfection, and joy that comes from this knowing.*

We realize this Spirit as we look out upon the stars of our galaxy. We see the order of the planets and their orbits, how they effortlessly travel through Outer Space. We see the seasons as they come and go, revealing to us the necessity of periods to lie dormant (*winter*), to withdraw in quietness and stillness to replenish our thoughts and clear our hearts of the foolishness and clamor of the human kind of consciousness, only to enjoy newness of Life (spring) as it emerges out from those times of reflection. These are the ways of Father God's infinite Intelligence. Our Divine Mind speaks to our thoughts to impart wisdom and understanding, eventually leading us to know who Father is and our Oneness with Father.

There is a Rhythm of Life that forms everything visible. It fills all things, determines the existence of all, and directs the activity of all. It is the Life and breath of all that is formed. IT is also referred to as the Spirit of the Life of all things. IT is the Law of Spirit and Life; IT is our Chi, which is our lifeforce, essence, and inner self. IT is our Holy Breath.

I no longer think the way I used to think; yes, the old thoughts try to sneak up on me, but all I need to do is replace them with the truth, and they flee. Now when I study the many Bible versions, I can look through the lens of love and see the underlying reality. Now I understand things I read in the Bible, which previously made no sense to me. What is most important to me now is to see all that I see the way Father God sees and the way Jesus saw all people and situations. Jesus saw what the Life of all things made and maintains through Father's eternal creative spiritual law giving and revealing activity. Father chose to see that which is unlimited in every person. Father sees Life everywhere, in everything.

Father would reveal to Man his genuine relationship with his Creator. Father would cause Man to see who they are in the eternal oneness of relationship with Father. Biblically this is called the "new creation," however, we are not new. We are eternal. We have always been and will always be one with Father. Father lives through us and demonstrates HIS marvelous nature as us. We are Father's abode. While this is referred to in many versions of the Bible as a "new" creation, it is the creation as it was known by the Divine Mind of Father from "before the foundation of the world." Creation never needed to become a new creation. Mankind only needs to take the dominion they have always had and restore order to it.

Father is with, in, and as you. Father is not a sense realm man that would lie. Father is already all things for which daily life requires. Father is jealous over you. Father is always love. Father is the Father of all people, and the Lord of lords, the great Father, and goes before you. The eternal Father is our refuge, and underneath you are the Everlasting Arms. The Lord, your Father, is with you wherever you go. Every place in Scripture where we read the phrase "Jesus is" speaks of the Father's character and Divine Nature Activity in Jesus and us.

**All thought, all understanding, all wisdom, all strength and all power comes from one Source, which is that of our Father within and without.**

Father is the Source of all joy, peace, perfection, and all life, seen and not seen with physical eyes. This idea of peace and perfection, or spiritual unity, wholeness, order, soundness, and completeness that gives peace, comes only from our Father within, and HE is our peace/perfection.

Life is Divine, and its Source is Father, Breath. IT does not originate only from the Soul but from the Source of the Soul. IT is neither a psychic nor purely mental activity nor springs from the physical. Our Source/Father is Breath (spirit), and one can be truly quickened with revitalizing life by consciously contacting their Divine Mind. When constant contact is made, seeming errors sink into nothingness. The error cannot withstand the almightiness, omnipresence, and omniscience of Father, the Source, the creative spiritual law giving and revealing activity in Man.

**The Book of Life:**

Although the Holy Scriptures are almost entirely considered the printed Bible only, the accurate Scriptures are the book of life within our Divine Mind, flowing to our conscious awareness. The written word is meant as a clue to a more vital part of the Scriptures than appears since they have both a literal and a spiritual significance.

The true meaning of the Bible is a divine "book of life" rather than merely a history of people, and it bears "witness unto the word of God (Acts 14:3). The word (logos), spiritually means the living, creative spiritual law-giving, and revealing activity of truth.

When we understand this power of the living, creative spiritual law-giving, and revealing activity of truth (Logos), we have the key to the imperishability of sacred writings. According to tradition, all the papers of the Hebrew Bible were destroyed; but they were restored by Esdras, who remembered in his awareness and rewrote them. Modern discoveries in the realm of understanding explain in a measure this spiritual statement. We know now that every word that man utters makes an imprint in the spiritual atmosphere. Where there is the consciousness of God-life in the Divine Mind influenced consciousness awareness of the teacher/speaker, their words become living identities preserved throughout the ages. Anyone who develops sufficient spiritual power (understanding) may enter this book of life within the Divine Mind and spiritually read and teach out of its pages.

**Scribes:**

"Scribes represent the thoughts that come to us from our Source Father; Spirit inspires us from within. When Spirit speaks, no person can be quoted as authority--the Truth itself is authority, and it bows to no individual interpreter."

"For he (Jesus) taught them as having authority, not as the law writers."

**The Single-Eye:**

Mattew 6:22 The light of the body is the eye: if therefore, your eye is single, your whole awareness shall be full of light. Luke 11:34-36 The true spiritual wisdom, knowledge, and understanding of the Soul is the single eye: Therefore when your eye is single, your conscious awareness is also full of true wisdom, knowledge, and understanding; but when your eye is not spiritual (single), your conscious awareness is full of untruths and sense intellect. So, beware that the wisdom, knowledge, and understanding you have is not sensual intellect. Suppose your Soul, therefore, is full of spiritual wisdom, knowledge, and understanding, having no part that is sensual knowledge. In that case, the whole shall be full of wisdom, knowledge, and understanding, as when the bright shining of a candle doth give you light.

> Our Divine Mind is Fathers' Divine Mind. Our relationship with Father is much more than just a Son or Daughter. Why, because a Son or a Daughter can still see themselves as "less than Father." The many teachings of religiosity produce a "less than" mentality in their followers. We are the living, creative spiritual law-giving and revealing activity made a living Soul.*
>
> *The Word made a Soul.
>
> Next time someone ask who you are, say, "I am a living, creative spiritual law-giving and revealed activity living Soul."
>
> Facebook: Roy E. Richmond

Did you know to stop Luther and the Reformation, religiosity came up with an any-minute rapture of the faithful and eternal torment for the unfaithful to control the people?

The world's other systems have caught on to what fear will do. The political system is doing just that. Why? Because a person living in fear can be controlled. In like manner, a person trying to earn favor and the right to go to a better place also can be controlled. Father said, "Do not fear; you are always one with me and me with you." Paraphrased.

**You are the Light of your World:**

Are you aware that LIGHT is the understanding principle in our Divine Mind? Light is a symbol of wisdom. When Jesus said, "I am the light of the world" (John 8:12), he meant he was the expresser of Truth in all aspects.
Later, John wrote, "...I write unto you, which thing is true in Jesus and in you: because the lack of knowledge and wisdom (darkness) is passed, and the true LIGHT, who are people yielding their awareness to the higher understanding (Divine Mind), now shines. (1 John 2:8)
Let your Divine Wisdom and Understanding shine! Your world needs IT.

**The Spiritual understanding of Sheol:**

The day-to-day lower consciousness of the unawakened SOUL is Sheol. The lower awareness that people have adjusted is not meant for them to inhabit it. The antidote to the loss of awareness is simple: Father is in us as us; here, now, always, and we are One. "Rouse out of your stupor, to your accurate equity of character as Holy, don't miss the mark of who you are, or live in ignorance of the proper knowledge of Father: Some have not the true knowledge of Father, resulting in their confusion; to you, I speak." RERichmond Tree of Life Bible Translations

**You are the Duplicate of the Brethren:**

"Present yourselves as the duplicate of your brethren and revere them as Sons and Daughters of Father, just as you revere yourself as One with Father." Ephesians 5:21
In other words, "Don't speak bad of other people, no matter what awareness they are walking in."

**Contemplations of Ephesians 5:7-23:**

Ephesians 5:7, Do not listen to or dine on the empty words of teachers, who only proclaim the knowledge of good and bad; producing a strong sense of being void of your union with Father.
Verse 8, Previously, your awareness was not spiritual, and your understanding was darkened. Father, and even Jesus was a mystery to you; but now, after you embraced

what Jesus taught, and I have now explained to you, you understand you walk in the realm of actual spiritual substance and Life. You were not aware, but you are eternally intelligent (light) because you have Father's Divine Mind.
(Light is a symbol of intelligence; you are the Light of the World, so you can say, "I am intelligence; I am the Light of the World).

Verse 9, Your love nature being poured out on others, reveals your righteousness, virtue, goodness, and the not concealing Word you live by. 10 This flow of Life and Love agree with your creative being as a Son or Daughter of Father. 11 And deny any union with dead works of righteousness, which are not spiritual and lower your awareness of Father. I admonish you to reject those carnal thoughts and beliefs.

Verse 12, Even though some speak privately of dead works and false beliefs, with the resulting lifestyle, it would be a shame to speak ill of them. 13 Moreover, the whole of what they believe and promote, by Divine Intelligence being revealed in due time, will expose to them the falseness of what they believe. Let them be until the Intelligence (light) of Divine Revelation is embraced by them. 14 Wherefore, Father sayeth, awake, rouse from sitting or lying in disease, from no intimate knowledge of

Me; from a life of obscurity, inactivity, ruins, nonexistent. Arise in your awareness, from the lower conscious you lived in, and let the same Divine Mind that was in Jesus be active in you, and revealing to you that you are Divine Intelligence – you are a Son or Daughter of Father – the True Intelligence of the World.

Verse 15, In regard to you, likewise, just like Jesus walked, you walk not unwise, but wise with thoughts that radiate, bring understanding, spiritual satisfaction, and attentively listening to the Voice of Father speaking in your thoughts. 16 Do not be distracted by the seeming bad around you; missing out on hearing Father's Voice and not being a Voice to your world. 17 I say again, do not be ignorant of spiritual things but understand the purpose of Father for you. 18 And, do not give yourself entirely to carnal appetites and desires that lead to breaking up the whole consciousness, leading one to a confused and mixed state of consciousness; allow yourself to be overflowing with your Holy Breath.
19 Speak to yourselves of the truth of Father, in poetry or music, spiritually singing, with divine worship in your awareness of Father.
20 Be grateful always for the Way of life Jesus revealed and the eternal blessings of our Father. 21 Present yourself

as the duplicate of your brethren and revere them as Sons and Daughters of Father, just as you revere yourself as One with Father. 22 Allow your feminine phase awareness to be interpenetrated by the awareness of your inner Man – your Divine Mind. 23 For your Divine Mind is the Source of your conscious awareness.

**Adoption or Oneness?:**

I received a request on FB Messenger to explain Ephesians 4:1, with emphases on the word "adoption," as in "we were adopted into the family of Father" by "getting saved."

My answer: The phrase "adoption of children" should have been translated as "the place of a Son, just as Jesus was himself."

Ephesians 1:4: According, as he has chosen us in himself (Father), before the foundation of the world, that we exist holy and unblemished, with eyes wide open toward Him in a relation of rest and love: 5 Having predestinated, predetermined, decreed, declared, revealed us, a Son or Daughter, as Jesus was himself, according to the good pleasure of Fathers will. RERichmond Tree of Life Bible Translations

People were taught that they became holy and righteous only when Jesus resurrected, and they prayed a specific type of prayer. We were taught Jesus bore man's sin; then and only then did we become blameless.

The fact is you were always holy and unblemished with Father. The King James VERISON erroneously used the phrase "adoption of children," which implies a non-biological or non-spiritual union.

Paul was not telling the Believers at Ephesus they were adopted. He revealed that Jesus' passion revealed we were always Sons and Daughters. It was always Father's will to have Holy Sons and Daughters, and He got that in all people at the creation of Mankind. Father made us that way, and nothing can undo what Father Hath Done.

**Are we really to "fear" Father?**

Solomon finally figured it out. After approximately twelve years of lots of women, money, power, and philosophy, according to the "Authorized" King James Version, he said, "Let us hear the conclusion of the whole matter: Fear

God and keep his commandments: for this is the whole duty of man." (Eccl 12:13 KJV)

What he said, according to the corrected translation, is, "Let us hear the conclusion of the whole matter, intelligently hear Father, and revere our true Divine nature; for we are the whole and complete man." (Eccl. 12:13).

And from that time on, Solomon was known as "the preacher."

We must know and revere who we are. The word "fear" in much of the Scripture came from a word meaning revere.

**Do we have a Soul and Spirit, and do they need to be divided asunder?**

The King James Version of the Bible records Paul's book of Hebrews stating, "The word of God is sharper than any two-edged sword…., and able to divide asunder of soul and spirit…." Since the Soul and Spirit are the same, why would there need to be a "dividing asunder," as though our Soul is separate? It does not. The phrase "divide asunder" is from the Greek merismos (mer-is-mos'), which can be separation or distribution. Since the Soul and

Spirit are the same, the proper word would be distribution, as in, "The Word of God is powerful enough to distribute its Truth to every Soul."

**What needs "quickening" in us?**

The Quickening we need today is waking the whole Man to the full consciousness of what they are in the sight of Father our Source. The sense Man is only half-awake (dead to being in contact with Father), going about in a dream and thinking it is real life. The not concealed Word of Father is quick, and when it enters into Man's awareness, he stands upright on his feet, picturing his Divine understanding, and he knows and sees himself as he is. He is wide awake, alert, quick, and powerful. This transformation into vitalizing Spirit accomplishes Its work by adding to every Word a spiritual idea. The idea of "omnipresent" life will then quicken the physical life in Man, making conscious contact with the One life and drawing IT out for the benefit of the many. Hence, Apostle Paul meant when he wrote, "Be transformed by your renewing mind," which is your Divine Mind; IT ever regenerates, refreshes, and stimulates your brain, subconsciousness, and conscious awareness.

## What do we really need?

Our need is to feed on the Living Word of Truth, believe the Truth, embrace the Truth, and REMAIN in our awareness of Father by staying in contact with Father. Then, and only then, can we say we are not controlled by a consciousness that does not possess the knowledge of Father.

Our awareness has been born anew to its "original formation," meaning I remain in perfect Contact with my Father, Divine Mind, Source, and I know the whole of that which is complete: anything I need to know. Therefore, I have confidence in what I know and the Source of what I know and will continue to ascertain, seek and desire to believe that which I do not understand yet.

To be "born again" is to remember who I am and my awareness to be brought back to my original formation or foundation of Truth (made new). This reminds me of needing my computer hard drive "reformatted." What takes place at the reformation of the hard drive is there are still fragments left of files I initially deleted. Over years of use, those fragments slow the speed of my computer and even cause problems. The space these fragments took up is still impacted by them.

We could picture that of me sitting on my leather sofa. When I rise from the couch, there are wrinkles in the leather that came from my bottom sitting on it. To remove the wrinkles, I freshen (make new) the cushion, and there are no more wrinkles. It is our sub or inner consciousness that needs this reformatted, reviving Life.

**Do you know what "sin" is? Maybe not.**

"Rouse out of your stupor, to your accurate equity of character as Holy, don't miss the mark of who you are, or live in ignorance of the proper knowledge of Father: Some have not the true knowledge of Father, resulting in confusion, I speak. RERichmond Tree of Life Bible Translations and Paraphrasing

## Mary Magdalene and the Messenger at the Garden:

After Mary Magdalene ran to the garden to minister to Jesus' body, she saw the tomb was empty. She saw a Gardener and asked him if he knew where they had taken Jesus' body. When the person (Messenger) spoke as a Voice of One, she heard him as the Voice of One and wrongly thought it was Jesus. She called him "Teacher," and the person instructed her, saying, "Jesus? Not me! Do not attach yourself to me as if I were Jesus. Because of what Jesus has done, you can arise in your awareness of our Father: Go to the brothers near and far and say, as I said to you, rise in your understanding and awaken to the Father of All.

## Sin, is living with a mistaken identity, and following do to be laws to please Father:

There are two verse's in Scripture that state Jesus destroyed the Law of doing to be. The first is 1 John 3:8. The grossly translated King James Version states, "He that committeth sin is of the devil; for the devil sinneth from the beginning. For this purpose, the Son of God was manifested, that he might destroy the works of the devil." KJV

However, a more accurate translation and understanding is, 1 John 3:8 & 9, "He that identifies with a mistaken identity and seeks to please Father with many "do to be" works, is of the hindering and traducing Mosaic Law; for the Law produced the mistaken identity and dead works of righteousness from the beginning. For this was rendered apparent in that a Son of God, Jesus, loosened, put off, melted away, and brought to not the works of the traducing Mosaic Law.

1 John 3:9, For all people are procreated of the Father and are continually energized by their Divine Mind. So, if they embrace what Jesus taught and did, they will no longer live with a sense of separation, which is transgressing themselves, not Father. For Father's Holy Breath (seed) is in them and remaineth, and they cannot be separated from Father because they are born of and as Father in their entire being. RERichmond Tree of Life Bible Translations and Paraphrased.

**Are you aware everything you seek, spiritually and physically, exist already - for you to discover and experience?**

No one invented anything; it, whatever it was, already exist.

Electricity was always available, but not known until someone discovered it. Then more people came along and discovered more uses for electricity.

Even in the days of Moses and Abraham, electricity existed, but they were not aware. In the time of the Ancients, they discovered and built some, to us unbelievable structures and more, that amazes Man today. How you ask. They discovered principals that were already available to those who seek to know.

So, to, that which is spiritual / supernatural / physical already is.

Quit looking out there in the "sweet by and by," know what you seek is now in you and around you. Lift your awareness to spiritual understanding.

With calmness and quietness, ask to know and be aware of a thing or truth, and it will be revealed to you.

**To those who wonder what's going on, in your questioning your theology, know that you are loved and loveable.**

The only thing that's occurring is that old beliefs and awareness's are being released, and true awareness's and beliefs are replacing the old, that a new understanding of worthiness, peace, wakefulness, and oneness with Father and all creation might replace the old.

**Doing the right thing should not require receiving something back; Just Do It.**

**I have discovered, if one wants to hear Truth, in any system of this earth (religious, political, financial, medical, and social), they won't hear it where the "crowd mentality," feeds.**

**Were you taught about the city of On?**

On is a city Moses was trained in. On means; the city of the sun, the embodiment of light, luminous corporeity, radiating brilliance, the sun, faculty, ability, strength, power of radiation, wealth, and substance.

On is a city in Lower Egypt, one of the oldest known cities in the world. It is also called Heliopolis and Beth-shemesh. Heliopolis was devoted to the pure, monotheistic worship of a god that was symbolized in the sun. In its sanctuaries, Moses was educated as the foster son of Pharaoh's daughter as a prince and priest of Egypt. Homer, Plato, Pliny, and other sages of the Western world went to this city to obtain initiation into philosophy and cosmic mystery. Joseph's wife was the daughter of Potiphera, the priest of On (Gen. 41:45). (See Jeremiah 43:13) Aven, in Ezekiel 30:17, is said to refer to the city of On in Egypt.

Allegorically, in its purity, On refers to Spirit and to true spiritual understanding, substance, and power. As it appears in our Bible, however, the outer symbol (the sun) is worshiped and the truth back of the symbol has been lost to a great degree. This worshipping of the outer symbol, or form, and looking to the outer for understanding and all good is idolatry and must come to an end. We must stop studying Scripture from a surface-level understanding; it brings nothing but a sense of lack and death to the knowledge of the Father. That's why we learn and teach the Allegorical, Spiritual, Parabolical, Metaphorical, Metaphysical, and Symbolic meanings of all the Scripture. There is much truth to be discovered that is just below the surface of each word and sentence of your Bible. Job wrote, "There exists a great fountain of Life-

Force, within us, that reveals the awesomeness of true Redemption and Righteousness, and the decree of our Divine Nature is clarified."

**Did you know the word "spiritual" is used 29 times in the New Outlook and Perception Books?**

The word "spiritual" was translated from the Greek word "peneumatikos (pnyoo-mat-ik-os), which means "non-carnal." Peneumatikos comes from a root word meaning pneuma, which means "breath." The translators used "Spirit," which is a Latin word. Living Spiritually is to live as superhuman, which is living other than as mere humans. We are not human; we are Spirit and live spiritually (no-carnal).

**Did you know? There is no such word as "testament" in Hebrew, and in the Greek the word "testament" is there but it does not have "new" before it.**

The word "new" was added by the translators. Other places where they used the phrase, "of the new," it means freshness, not "new in a way that it has never been before."

I translate it as False or New Outlook and Perception Books.

When Jesus began to teach he tried to change the people's perception of Father and their selves, supposedly resulting in a new outlook of Life. Scripture states Father never changes, so why would there be an old and new covenant or testament? Only Man who lives by sense knowledges vacillates back and forth in their understanding.

**Have you wondered where Enoch went, where the Scripture said, "And Enoch walked with God: and he was not; for God took him" (Genesis 5:24), and "God had translated him?" (Hebrews 11:5)**

ENOCH – Chanowk (khan-oke') meaning initiated, founder, centralizer, teacher, and fixer.

Allegorically, Enoch's name infers an entrance into and instruction in a new state of thought of understanding. In the case of Enoch, who walked with God (lived out of the Spirit (Holy Breath – ruwach – cool of the day), the new state of thought would be spiritual consciousness, the new life in constant contact with his Divine Mind – Father.

Likely many of us, at the time of my writing, are experiencing what Enoch's name means, "Entrance into a higher consciousness that has been known and experienced before by many." Enoch went within to seek "THE" greater awareness.

Could we say he fully awakened to who he was and most likely translated somewhere out of the sight of those with him? There are many records in Scripture and other writings that people have translated at one time or another. For those who were not spiritually aware, they would say, "Oh, God took him," just like they did Jesus. Jesus had translated several times while in Jerusalem and the surrounding area; there is no reason to think he did not translate to other places when he left his disciples. Why would I believe that? Because he appeared to the disciples several times and taught them, he appeared to Paul and taught him, and he appeared to John and taught him. Could it be that Jesus is still instructing people, and they do not know it is Jesus?

Hebrew 13:2 states, "Be not forgetful to entertain people you don't know: for thereby some have been the host of Messengers unaware."

Phillip translated after he baptized a Eunuch; Elijah, Phillip, and many others have translated.

**Who was Adam? One man or a race of Man?**

Adam – (aw-dawm") OT:120 Adam ruddy. From OT:229 'adam – to show blood in the face. The name of the first race of Mankind, used in the King James Version and other versions as the first man, as an individual.

Metaphorically, Adam' symbolizes the first movement of the Divine Mind, in IT's CONTACT with life and substance. Adam' also represents the entire race of Mankind, embodied in an individual- Man idea. Eve is the feminine aspect of universal Man, outwardly manifest: "So, created Father, Man as a representative figure in resemblance, Father created Male and Female to create Father in a body, everlastingly." RERichmond Tree of Life Bible Translations

Adam' in their original creation were in spiritual illumination. Holy Breath breathed into them continually the necessary inspiration and knowledge to give them superior understanding. But they began eating, or appropriating, ideas of two powers--God and not God, or good and bad. The allegory relates to the result was that they fell away, in their awareness from spiritual life and all that it involves. However, they continued to be Spirit, but they forgot who they were.

Mankind is Spirit (Holy Breath), absolute and unconditional; but Man forms an Adamic consciousness into which they breathe the breath of life; this, in its perfect expression, is the or a Son of man, an expression of the Divine idea. This Adam' is all of what we term soul, intellect, and body as One. We who are awakened to greater truth, are continually at work with this Adam' race; we can breathe into their nostrils the breath of life, inspiring them with the Divine idea of life in all its unlimited fullness. We can lift up this Adam' race by infusing into them these sublime ideas, and in no other way. How do we do this? As we ascertain, seek and desire to know Father, in us as us, we do so in a position of being Holy Breath, and we know Truth is within us – we hear the Voice of One in our thoughts, and we only say what we hear Father say.

"What we now know is a drop; what we don't know and can know is an Ocean.

Far too many people are stuck in the drop, defend the drop and make denominations around the drop.

We must wade out deep in the Ocean of Revelation and see where it brings us. You might see the light of Glory in a way you've never seen IT."

**Does Father need appeasement from Mankind?**

In 1st Chronicles 4:16, there was a man named Ishbah (ish'-bah), whose name, in Hebrew, means Father will tell the story, Father will glorify, Father will soothe, Father, will appease, and Father will still the turmoil. Ishbah was the father of Eshetmoa, of the tribe of Judah. An example of Ishbah would be when we know the true character and nature of our Father, and when we tell the true story (praise) concerning Father, then we experience the activity of our Holy Breath in our consciousness, which very quickly releases a calm and quiet state of awareness in us. In this state of calm and quiet, we realize our Father's true character and nature and experience a strong sense of inner peace and satisfaction that it is Father soothing and stilling us. We no longer live with a false sense of needing to appease Father. Father needs no appeasement, never has, and never will.

**What if Jesus allowed the Pharisees and Roman soldiers to kill him, was because he knew it was time to leave the people?**

Why? So that Father and he could equip another Comforter Messenger Teacher (Paul) to come on the scene and explain what Jesus tried to instruct the people of his world and for all generations after? The people only saw Jesus as a rescuer of their seeming lack and, therefore, would not intelligently listen to what he came to them to teach.

As long as Jesus was present in his body, all the people wanted was physical miracles and help. If he had stayed, they would have continued to seek him for temporal help, and they would live their entire life "in need."

Western Evangelical Christianity has taught people to do the same thing; seek Jesus for help in what their strong sense of lack and the experience of that false lack wants.

If we would get past the barrier in our awareness that holds us back, we could awaken to our Oneness with Father and "come up hither," which means to rise higher in our Spiritual awareness.

Rather than asking Jesus to do something for us, we need to ascertain, seek and desire to know Father in Spirit and truth, and not seek for Jesus to do something for us. Father seeks those people who seek to know HIM and, in turn, know themselves for who they are. "Praying in Jesus' name" means praying in the exact nature and the way Jesus did - converse the Truth over people and every situation.

The King James VERSION of our bible records Jesus saying, "Ask anything, and you shall receive." The English word "ask" was translated from a Greek word that means "Ascertain, seek and desire to know…," not to ask for a thing, and so forth.

People have often asked me why they can't get their prayers answered. Maybe we are praying amiss, always asking for something, rather than seeking to know Father in greater awareness and who we really are.

An intimate relationship with Father negates the need to ask for things. Selah

You ask, "What's the barrier?" The barrier, traducer and hindered, is this same thing Jesus dealt with - any law of "doing to be" who you already are. The wall includes our firmly held beliefs in what religiosity has taught us. We fight for what hinders us.

It's time to let go; your world needs you to be a Comforter Messenger of the truthful Word to them.

**I talked with a long-time friend; we discussed what we believed concerning the scripture, Father, Jesus, and ourselves.**

Just now, I began to think about believing and knowing; there is a big difference between the two. I told my friend there are some greater understandings that I know.

There was a time in history when a man brought his son to the Great Comforter Teacher Jesus. The man asked Jesus if he would heal his son. Jesus replied to him, "I will do you believe?" He had heard of or seen Jesus restore people's health, so based on what he saw, he said, "Yes, I believe...." And, of course, the child was restored to health.

But that was not all the man said. He continued, "... but help me in my unbelief." A few years ago, I sought the meaning behind what he said. I heard in my thoughts, from Father's voice, "Help me in what I don't know to believe." Therefore, knowing something is better than just believing.

You might believe something about me that is not true. What you think can be based on false perceptions or something you've heard about me that is untrue. But if you know me, then what you believe of me is based on facts.

So, knowing is vital for all of us. Father seeks those who ascertain, seek, and desire to KNOW Father in Holy Breath (spirit -a Latin word) and Truth. This is the reason I am a seeker of the not-concealed (Truth) Word. I'm no longer interested in studying the textual interpretation and the study of the scriptures. I'm searching for the spiritual, allegorical, parabolical, and mystical understanding of every word, verse, and story.

I don't want to believe something; I want to know that I know before I share the Real Good News, which is the Gospel of Oneness and Fathers' eternal love, with no requirements.

**I was involved in a posting conversation, and many of those posting were discussing "casting out devils."**

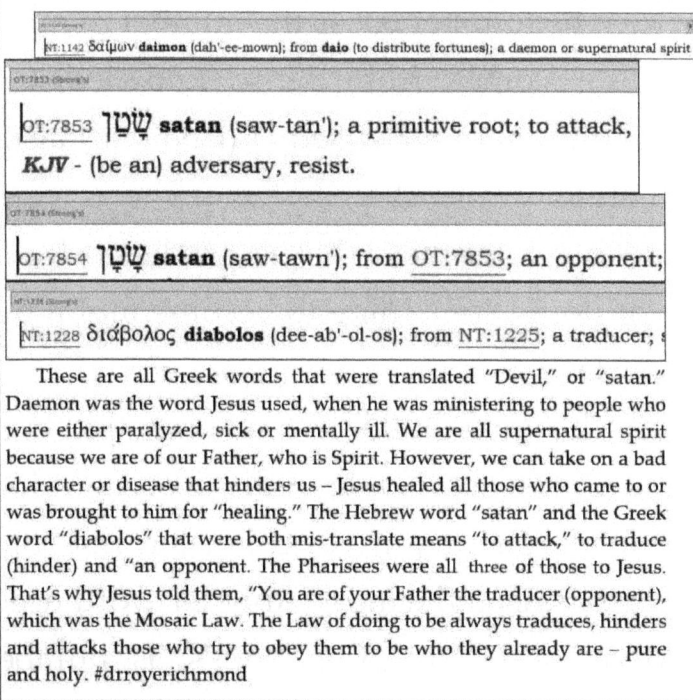

**It is interesting to study the meanings of the word "righteousness," in the Hebrew, which was the language of the Old Outlook and Perception books, and the Greek meaning in what was supposed to be the New Outlook and Perception books.**

In the Old Outlook books, the Hebrew word that was translated an English word – righteousness, is the number 6666 tsedaqah (tsed-aw-kay), meaning rightness in a moral sense. The number 666 is the number of man whose understanding comes from sense knowledge – dust dwellers. The number 6664 tsedeq (tseh'dek) also means right in a natural or moral sense.
Both would be a rightness that is produced by living a moral life or doing something to become moral by an act or obeying a law.
However, in the New Outlook and Perception books, the word is the Greek number 1343 dikaiosune (dik-ah-yos-oo'-nay), meaning an equity of character; not something to earn, which is used the most. Another word used in the New Outlook and Perception books, is number 1342 dikaios, meaning equitable, implying innocent and holy – something you are created as, not something you earn.

One other word for righteousness, is found in Hebrews 1:8, recording Jesus saying, "Father is the power or Source (scepter) of righteousness and the power Source of the Kingdom." The English word righteousness here, came from Greek number 2118, meaning rectitude, which is morally correct behavior or thinking.

Father is the Source of morally correct behavior or thinking, not rules, regulations or any kind of do to be laws.

**A short letter from Apostle Paul:**

Haven't you become aware that when you seek to listen and obey the Mosaic law, you become servants to every jot and tittle, and you allow yourself to become prey to the never-ending reliance upon its dead works of righteousness in your life and the mortal-mindedness it inflicts? What do you prefer, laws and dead works of righteousness, which produce nothing except a state of death, hopelessness, and the ever-spiraling death? Or do you choose to listen intelligently to my Voice of wisdom concerning your eternal righteousness, holy and equitable character, and nature, with which you were born? You, along with all people, have the right to this from the foundation of the world, but because you did not know, you did not possess or handle your righteousness and holiness and the supernatural life that is always yours.

I am so thankful that we are no more servants to the dictates of the Mosaic law and the dead works they produced. I have listened, with intelligence, to the Voice of Spirit, explaining what Jesus revealed in his incarnational events. The Voice has spoken concerning Father's eternal, great, and marvelous love for all people. Jesus first explained and delivered it to me. Now I am anointed to explain this marvelous unveiling of truth to you, as many more Comforter Messenger will explain in the future, age after age, world without end. It is a form of doctrine, using Jesus, our Master Comforter Teacher, as the extraordinary form of us all. He lived as who we are eternal. You can understand what I write to you, with intelligence and understanding, and hear the Voice of Holy Breath in yourself saying, "Amen"!

Sincerely, your fellow brethren, Paul.

**The majority of my life, I believed** to be the most important thing Jesus did, was die for mankind. No, he died because the religious leaders hated him. Now that

I'm a seeker of spiritual truths of the Scriptures and Jesus' teachings, I believe the most important thing Jesus did, is he lived for mankind and revealed the true way of life. Selah

In my younger years, I've often heard, "Make a wish upon a star, and you will receive your wish."

Donna was watching a movie today, and I heard that song being sung when Tom Hanks wished for Pinocchio to be turned into a real boy to be his actual son.

I heard in my thoughts, "Find a Star Teacher, and you will discover all you've dreamed of for your life and experience being a Son or a Daughter of God (Father).

A Star Teacher causes you to look up. A Star Teacher causes you to look up.

**For many years, I have been a spiritual mentor and teacher to thousands of people around this planet.**

I enjoy answering the many questions. However, at some point in the relationship, I give the exact instructions to each being mentored. I tell them it is time to move on from the "What about this and what about that" stage, study the material I've sent you, and watch the video teachings on my YouTube channel.

For most of those I mentor, I send them the PDF files of "No Penal Substitution," which Dr. Kay and I wrote, and other books of mine. I ask, "Have you read the books yet?" The answer is often,
Not yet," or "I've read several chapters."

Several years ago, I sat in a minister's office, talking about what I had learned from studying the materials provided to us by a Pastor we followed in ministry. This Pastor did not understand what I learned from studying what my mentor shared with me and often questioned my understanding. I looked behind my friend, and all of the Tape sets of our then Pastor were neatly arranged on the bookshelf. I asked, "Have you listened to any of those?" The answer was "no." I then understood the many questions because this minister did what the young disciple Timothy had done with Paul. Timothy constantly asked his mentor Paul, "What about this and what about that?"

When you attended school or college, a good teacher or professor would not answer all your questions; they would tell you to read the books and study. The Apostle Paul did the same to Timothy. Timothy was a young man (a teenager) at that time.

Why would a good Teacher, Professor or Messenger not answer all your questions? Because when it's time for the test, it's not the answers to the questions that will help you pass; it's how you come up with the answers that help you pass the test.

Paul told Timothy, "Study, to show yourself acceptable to Father, a student of the not-concealed Word needeth not to be ashamed, rightly dividing the word of truth (the not-concealed Word) himself." 2 Timothy 2:15

Moral of the story: If your mentor has recorded what they have learned in the many years of their study and lifetime, intently read the books, listen to their teachings, listen to the Voice of Father in your thoughts, and know and understand what they learned and build upon that. Then, you will know the answers and see how studying the "God-inspired" Scriptures equips you to discover the answers.

If you follow my teachings and/or I mentor you, please continue with your questions; for the sake of those, you will share with, read, and study the books - not just one time but many. You need much more than the answers; you need to see, know, understand and embrace the answers that will "make you free" and those you will mentor.

As always, I love, respect, and value all of you. I feel your conversations for Divine health and strength overshadow me and that I will always hear the Voice of Father in my thoughts as I study and teach. Never go back - you're on a journey to the high place of tasting and seeing that our Father is eternally good.
Selah

**What do people need the most to succeed in any endeavor? Confidence!**

Romans 4:11-24, the Apostle Paul wrote much about the confidence of Abraham and then ended the chapter in verse 25, writing about Jesus' confidence.

Spiritual confidence comes from a state of thought that is continually searching after the eternal ideas of the Father and endeavors to gain spiritual knowledge and understanding by every means possible. They are not stuck in one particular religion or one that was good enough for "grandmother." There is a fishing town near the Sea of Galilee named Bethsaida. Bethsaida means house of fishing, place of hunting, place of nets, fishing town, and hunting town. Thus, Bethsaida spiritually speaks a consciousness of an increase of ideas.

In Mark 8:22, we read of when a blind man was brought to Jesus to be healed. Metaphorically, the blind man represents a darkened awareness. When we are exalted in consciousness, the darkness or lack of understanding disappears; revelatory light always swallows the darkness. As we embrace the light, we experience the realization in consciousness that our life is being constantly awakened (made new) by the activity of our Divine Mind being allowed to influence every part of our being. A great picture of contact with our Divine Mind is the purification and upbuilding of our blood by coming in contact with the oxygen of the air in our lungs. In a sense, the blood becomes new again.

**I often hear in my thoughts the song Beulah Land.**
Often Beulah Land was sang at my child-hood Church.
Do any of you remember this song?

I'm kind of homesick for a country
To which I've never been before.
No sad goodbyes will there be spoken
For time won't matter anymore.
Beulah Land (Beulah Land) I'm longing for you (I'm longing for you)
And someday (And someday) on thee I'll stand (Someday we will stand)
There my home (There my home) shall be eternal (Eternal)
Beulah Land, sweet Beulah Land
I'm looking now, just across the river
To where my faith, shall end in sight (Shall end in sight)
There are just a few more days to labor.
Then I will take my heavenly flight.
Beulah Land (Beulah Land) I'm longing for you (I'm longing for you)
And someday (And someday) on thee I'll stand (Someday we will stand)
There my home (There my home) shall be eternal
Beulah Land, sweet Beulah Land

Beulah Land, oh it's Beulah Land
Oh, Beulah Land, sweet Beulah Land

In the Bible, the Hebrew meaning of Beulah is married. Physically, Beulah was a name given by Isaiah to the land and nation of Israel, signifying the perfect union with Father, to which the Israelites would return.

Other than physically (Spiritually), the Allegorical meaning of Beulah is the rich and happy state of the individual who has entered into conscious union with the Divine; or one in whom the marriage of the Lamb has taken place, which symbolizes the raising of the whole consciousness to perfect and complete oneness with the Father or indwelling contact with the Divine Mind (Father). We also speak of the "marriage of the Lamb" as the lifting up and unifying of wisdom and love in individual consciousness. When this spiritual marriage occurs, the individual's condition is blessed, prosperous, and complete.

**I think often about the need for many more, "Comforter Messengers," in our present world.**

It is plain to any unbiased awareness that Jesus of Nazareth was a religious reformer with a mission from on high. He had an insight into those things which are ever mysteries to people immersed in the sense consciousness. Through his knowledge and in harmony with his mission, he set into motion spiritual ideas that, ever since his ministry, have been operative in the world. It is evident to even a superficial reader of his life and teachings that he was a Comforter Messenger of a thoroughly organized plan to help mankind into a higher realization of Father and their relation to their Source Father.

There are many more Comforter Messengers in our present time who are grinding out the Word to make it palatable to the reader; their plan is also to help mankind into a higher realization of the Father and their relation to their Source Father.

**Do you know what the word, Mercy, means, other than the English Answers? No? Then I will show you.**

Here is a list of words translated as "Mercy": Hebrew #2617 checed, which means kindness, beauty, to and to bow in courtesy to an equal. I like that because Hosea says,

"We exist as the plural of Father. Next is Hebrews #7356 racham, compassion, as in cherishing a fetus in the womb. Next, Hebrew #2603, as in showing mercy, is Chanan, meaning to bend or stoop in kindness and graciousness, and showing favor (favor means image; as my son favors me). In every Scripture in the OT that states, "Oh give thank for the Lord, for his mercy endureth for ever;" the phrase "endureth forever" is always added by the translators. The writer just said, "Oh, give thanks for the Lord, for his kindness, beauty, seeing us as an equal, and cherishing us as His Sons and Daughters." Father does not have to "endure us."

Now the Greek language - NT:1653 eleeo, to be compassionate, as in caring. And then we find NT:3629 oiktirmon - also meaning compassionate, and the root word is oikteiro, meaning to exercise pity.

The Oxford dictionary gives the following definition of the English word "Mercy." "Compassion or forgiveness is shown toward someone whom it is within one's power to punish or harm." That could never be the meaning of Father's racham, chanana, checed because, within Father, there is nothing in Father that would punish or harm anyone. That's why I do not use "mercy" when thanking Father for his relationship with me or others. If you remember, before Jesus brought people back to their right mind or restored them physically, scripture always said, "And he had compassion on them..." The reason the modern Church is not bringing people to their right mind or healing them is that we really have not seen them with compassionate eyes (the single eye).

The phrase used for Jesus, "He had compassion," is in the snippet below of my bible program.

We need to know, without any doubt, that Father has no power in "him" to harm, hurt or punish anyone. If you believe Father does, the "god" you believe in is a false god made up by religiosity. Selah

NT:4697 σπλαγχνίζομαι **splagchnizomai** (splangkh-nid'-zom-ahee); middle voice from NT:4698; to have the bowels yearn, i.e. (figuratively) feel sympathy, to pity:
**KJV** - have (be moved with) compassion.

Matthew 6:9-12, commonly titled "The Lord's Prayer." Jesus did not need to pray this prayer; he showed the people around him how to talk with Father.

Matthew 6:9-12 Father, we are one in perfect rest, as you are Breath, we are Breath; holy and pure is our way and nature. Your nature and way is apparent in and as us. Our righteousness was caused to be from the foundation by your determination, decree, and purposed by you; in that same manner from the foundation, it is eternally true of everyone. That which is required daily is supplied. Our substances are bestowed day after day. Also, you send forth our belief of needing to appease you; in the same manner, we send forth that sense of needing others to appease us.

**Several years ago, I was in a discussion about why many people raised in Western Evangelical Christian Religions "unconsciously" prefer Jesus over Father.**

As I talked, I immediately heard, "It is because they put Jesus in the Mother's place, of an earthly Father and Mother relationship." I thought, "Wow, that's it!"

Almost all children prefer their Mother over their Father because their Mother is the one who cuddles them, comforts them when they are hurt, cooks meals for them, and so forth. Father? He is the one "Who will spank you when he gets home when you've done something wrong." Father loves you but is portrayed as more of an authoritative figure in the family unit.

(Yes, I know Father and Mother relationships have changed a lot in our day, but I'm using this as a physical picture of spiritual truth.)

Our many versions of the Word of God project the same between our Eternal Father and Jesus. The many Bible translations show Jesus as a "Provider when you have a need; comforter when you are hurting; Counselor when you need advice, and rescuer when you are in trouble."

Father? The Bible translations reveal Father as "wrathful," "angry," often filled with "indignation," and if you do not follow His rules, you will suffer on earth, and after you die (all not true), but don't forget, Father loves you!

Jesus came to reveal the true character and nature of the Father by showing us Father in him and telling us we have Father in us. Jesus never wanted us to make statues of him, the cross's with him hanging on them, and hang a picture on our walls that we think looks like him. Jesus never portrayed Father as needing to be feared by anyone. Jesus always said what he heard Father say, which was nothing but love, and he always did what he saw Father do: love for ALL people.

**Romans 2:12-16 - "Conscious Harmony."**

Some synonyms for "conscious" are: Sensible; Deliberate; Mindful; Determined; Intentional.

Our ministry name, Tree of Life Ministries, was a title we started in 1988. I've used it for many years, and it is listed worldwide on many social media platforms and our web page. However, today I see our many followers and us as many-membered people who are a fellowship of Conscious Harmony. I exist to facilitate the spiritual journey for people who want to "make contact" with Father (our Divine Mind) at the center of their lives while living in this world. We currently do that for thousands of people all around this planet. We intend to provide teachings of the Truthful Living Word, required for individuals to grow in a perfect conscious awareness, which eradicates the false belief of separateness from Father, and a separate existence apart from one another and Father. I desire to fully bring an enlightened experience of conscious union with our eternal Source

Father to everyone who hungers and thirsts for the Truth. When believed and embraced, what they know will bring them the experience of perfect oneness with Father.

So, what do I mean by Conscious harmony? Whenever you work in harmony with the Divine Principle (Father-Source), you will ally yourself with the Universe's great and only Force: the One who created all things seen and not yet seen. So many people are not living at peace with one another because they are not consciously living in harmony with Father. There is a better way to live with others, and it has to do with conscious harmony. Just like music, if you are in an orchestra, playing the violin, and you consistently choose to play a flat note when everyone is playing a sharp note or play a different note altogether, you will not be in harmony with the entire orchestra, and the whole song will sound terrible. That is happening today and has been for thousands of years. A world out of harmony is not a lovely place to live, but we can be those who usher in harmony needed in our world. It just takes a bit of fine-tuning.

One of our first understandings is that happiness appears when what we believe to be our outer enters into harmony with the Inward Man of our awareness (heart). Paul wrote in Romans 7:21, "For I delight in the law of God after the inward man." KJV

**I see many people post on Facebook the quote of Jesus saying, "The truth will set you free."**

One word is wrong in the quote; it's the word "set." Jesus actually used the phrase, "Make you free."

You say, "What's the difference?"

There is a big difference.

A long time ago, a man owned a bird and kept it in a cage (religiosity). The bird never knew any other life but the cage.

One day, the bird's owner decided to SET the bird free. The owner opened the cage so the bird could come out and soar in the sky. However, the bird would not come out because the cage was all it knew; it was afraid to come out.

Finally, after many tries of encouraging the bird to come out, he gently reached his hand in and took the bird out to the perch on the cage. After a few times, the bird returned to the cage, and the owner pulled it out and shut the cage door. Finally, the bird was MADE free and flew away to EXPERIENCE its newly discovered Life.

Jesus set his world, and hopefully you, free from the many laws of doing to be a false perception of Father and ourselves. When one hears and embraces the Truth, which came from a Greek word that means "not-concealed Word," they are MADE free, pointing to experience and raised in their awareness of their oneness with Father and the abundant life they always had.
Selah

**Your True Image**

Romans 2:10 Be aware now of this great valuable truth. The true condition of all mankind is they have quietness, rest, perfection, and peace, and they have been established eternally at one with Father. They are betrothed in the goodness of Father, including all the Jewish and the non-Jewish people. 11 Either way, we all exist (appear) as Father – we are the image of our Father. RERichmond Tree of Life Bible Translations

It is vital for everyone to understand the word "image" because there are many false images in the world that are projected into the awareness of people. I would guess that

99.99999999% of all people born quickly forget who they are and where they came from. Why would they forget being a Son or Daughter of Father God? It is because their parents, grandparents, and teachers of all forms did not teach them who they really were – the image of Father. We were taught our ethnicity and other images that do not conform to our real selves. Mankind unifies himself with Father (our Source) through recognition that he or she is a son or daughter, and heir of the Father, in whose image and likeness they were created. By realizing their Divine Mind, he or she becomes aware of their eternal oneness with and as Father.

For thousands of years, mankind has made all kinds of images of the Father and of themselves. Graven images of stone to bow down to, images of people, graven images in the likeness of male, female, and other things to bow down to, and many more false images to bow their thoughts and life to.

When we recognize this truth of us being the perfect image of Father, by means of the will, we give up our mortal images and ideas of ourselves and consecrate ourselves with all our faculties to spiritual expression; then our Holy Breath in us replaces the sensual ideas and images. We are, in truth, Spiritual, and we function naturally only when we function spiritually. We should not relate to any religion, race, or national title – we are spiritual.

**Are you aware you feel good not because the world is right, but your world is right because you feel good?**

"Every spiritual seeker (Mystic), who has found personal peace and happiness, has been through everything you may now be experiencing. He or she knows the barriers and the frustrations you face along the way. They understand your concern over financial affairs and know how fervently you wish you had not made that impulsive error; they see your secret sorrow. But these spiritual seekers (Mystics) know something far above all this. They know it can end because they have no power to make you feel bad.

Could you keep the following facts in your awareness?

1. Your world turns right when you feel right. 2. A clear understanding of negative emotions dismisses them. Work for their dismissal. 3. It is right and necessary to rebel constructively against tyrannical feelings within

yourself. 4. There is not a single painful mood that you cannot separate from your life.

5. It is essential to gain awareness of the whole process of desire. 6. Your true nature, which can continually be reclaimed, is free of painful cravings. 7. When we wake up to the facts of life, we are left with beneficial desires only. 8. Never condemn yourself for having negative emotions. Instead, find freedom through self-knowledge. 9. It is a fact you can be happy in the here and now."

**HOW TO DETACH DISTRESS and regain our natural and spontaneous feeling for life?**

From my study of writings of Ancient Comforter Messenger Teachers, with some additions of mine.

(Note: when I use the word "he," I am implying no gender. If you have followed my many post and teachings, you will recall me often saying, "Feelings can lie to you.)

"The detachment comes from the dynamic principles of the Spiritual Path, like this startling one: You have never been discouraged or depressed. You never have and never will make a mistake of any kind. The clue is in the word "you." As we have seen, man's real difficulty lies in his false identity. He wrongly takes himself as the negative false person (awareness). But, in reality, he is his True Self, that in no way can be damaging.

Here is how the mistake proceeds in a man's emotional life: A feeling of sadness arises. The man immediately identifies with it; he takes himself as the feeling. He thinks he is this feeling, which he is not. He doubles the error every time he says, I am sad. The more he says it, the more miserable he feels; the more pain he feels, the more he says it. If you run into this, what can you do? Separate the way you feel from who you really are. You are not that feeling of sadness.

Try to grasp this. Impersonalize a negative feeling. Do not say "I" to it. Instead, refer to the feeling as it. A man should say, It is depressed, it feels helpless, it is enslaved by passion, it feels guilty, it craves alcohol, it wants revenge, it is terrified, it is a compulsive eater, it has heartache, it feels betrayed, it is confused, it does foolish things, it is secretly bitter, it is envious, it feels bored, it is nervous, it has anxiety, it has sleepless nights, it is irritable, it is exhausted, and so forth.

Do you see what this does? It separates the false you from the real you. By detaching this false sense of identity, you also detach the distress it creates. Separate you're feelings about yourself from who you really are, a free person. Separate, separate, separate.

It is not an evasion of your responsibility when you attribute your negativities to "it." It is a new self-responsibility, a genuine technique that delivers you once and for all. Your whole duty is to understand this. It is your understanding that destroys painful negativities. Work with this miracle method of the Spiritual Path, and you will free yourself from lying feelings and continue to experience the cool of the day (spiritual life) as the person you are." Selah

**Every person is a king through conscious awareness of his true identity.**

They need not try to be anything; they need only realize who he really is, king by birthright. How can we start practicing this idea? How would you feel if you had no fear? Feel like that. How would you behave toward others if you realized their powerlessness to hurt you? Behave like that. How would you react to so-called misfortune if you saw its inability to bother you? Could you respond like that? What would you think about yourself if you knew you were all right? Think like that. These are kingly states of consciousness. By living with them, you live like a king.

We do not know Who we are because we are unaware that the Kingdom of Heaven is within us, that we behave in the generally silly, the often insane, the sometimes criminal ways that are so characteristically living in a state of being a "mere human. We experience the freedom of no fear and no threat when we are liberated and enlightened by perceiving the often unperceived Life Force that is already within us, by returning to our eternal Ground and remaining where, without knowing it, we have always been.

**I'm proud to be a "Believer" and an "American."**

We are still independent and can think "on" what is true. Carnal facts may say differently, but the Truth is what we must believe and live from.

Apostle Paul wrote to the Community of Believers at Philippi, saying, "Finally, family, whatsoever things are TRUE (not carnal facts), whatsoever things are honest, whatsoever things are just, whatsoever things are pure, whatsoever things are lovely, whatsoever things are of good report; if there be any virtue, and if there be any praise; think on these things." (Philippians 4:8)

Pastor Garner once said, "When you come to a place where they are teaching you, be sure to bring your brain.

**What is Truth?  The not-concealed, creative spiritual law giving and revealing activity in you (LOGOS).**

Truth - The Absolute; that which accords with Father as a divine principle; that which is, has been, and ever will be; that which eternally is.

The Truth of Father/Source/God is reality: "The same yesterday and today, surely and forever." The realities of being are eternal and have always existed. Truth abides in fullness at the very core of mankind's being. As their consciousness (awareness) expands, they touch the everlasting Truth. What seems new is the unveiling of what has always been and always will be.

The basic principle of Truth is that the conscious awareness of each individual may be consciously unified with Divine Mind through Contact with Father. By affirming at-one-ment with God-Mind, we eventually realize that perfect mind, which was in Christ Jesus, and according to the Apostle John, we should be aware that the same Divine Mind is in us; we only need to "let IT be."

Truth is the straight and narrow path, along which our Holy Breath moment-by-moment direction, and which proves so smooth and safe that one refuses to allow oneself to be misled by habit into trusting sense perception. If we listen, we can always hear The Voice of Father (Breath) that says, "This is the way; walk you in it." If one follows the path, the road will be smooth and safe. This, my friends, is the answer to one's prayers of safety, protection, eternal health, and daily supply.

## Who do I Exist as?

Over the last few years, many Doctors asked me to tell them who I am. The question was asked again in the recent past, but this time the question came from our Father through my thoughts. "Who are you?"

I've learned when one hears a question and knows it's from Father, the answer is forthcoming from Father.

I immediately heard this: "You are a follower of the Light (wisdom, knowledge, and understanding); You have become a Mystic, a seeker of spiritual truth. You have left behind carnal thoughts of need and desire, and the Light is lifting you higher. You are now entering the light with such a passion that, subjectively, you are being the wisdom, knowledge, and understanding (light) of your world. You are a Messenger of My truth, so go forth as the light you are. You know the Light, so follow IT, for It will not lead you to darkness."

Sincerely, Papa

It is so good to hear the Voice of our Father/Source/God and breathe the breath of our Father Creator. All of you need to know objectively that you are the light of the world; it's time for you to subjectively become the light of the world in your world. Why? Because they need your Divine wisdom, knowledge, and understanding that comes from you as a Book of Life.

While Jesus was in his world (Jerusalem and the surrounding area), he was both Objectively and Subjectively the Light of the World; he was the only one at the time who was Subjectively (personally) true wisdom, knowledge, and understanding. No one in his day possessed the inner light within them.

The Apostle John, speaking of mankind, said, "What was true in Jesus is true in you (all people), and he ended his statement by saying, "and the TRUE light now shineth." John used the same Greek word Jesus used in "The truth will make you free," which was translated as "true" from althes, meaning "the not concealing Light," meaning the cover was removed, and now our light can shine bright. What was concealed by religiosity was spiritual wisdom, knowledge, and understanding.

As always, I love you all!

**Did you know marriage is eternal?**

No writing of ordnance or man-made decree can break a true marriage.

Father said to the children of Israel, "I am married (one with) to the Cherubim (the people)." No matter what a person says from carnal (sense knowledge), nothing can separate you from your marriage (oneness) with Father. You are eternal, securely one - Married.

**The cause of self-condemnation.**

Romans 2:1 Therefore, they had no defense or excuse. They lived as mere humans (earthbound – hewn down), condemning others in their intensification of deciding against one another. They made decisions against themselves since they did the same things, for which they condemned others." RERichmond Tree of Life Bible Translations

It is time to break free from Self-condemnation.

**A long, long, long time ago, in a city named Rome, the following section of a letter was written to various groups of people, and for generation after generation.**

Now we know all mankind eternally had and has the benefit of being able to receive from the Voice of our Holy Breath, apart from the shedding of the blood of those sacrifices. We have the revelation, which Jesus revealed, concerning the truth about the eternal love of our Father towards us all. That revelation brought an end to the unnecessary bloody dead animal sacrifices. It showed us that the power of death was removed. The eternal laws of "doing to be" gave death its power. Now we fully live as Sons and Daughters of Father because we are rid of the mindset of wrongdoing. No longer do we have to contend with the sacrificial offerings to appease Father. We no longer have a slave mindset.

The intensification of our daily experience NOW is living eternally whole, well off, free, safe, and preserved because our confidence is in what Jesus came to reveal to the whole of humanity, and in the faith of our Father. Furthermore, if a person is aware of the truths Jesus sought to teach, then there would be no need for them to expect a future event that would render Holy Breath our life to become more apparent to them. If a person sees and is fully aware of the eternal life we possess, then nothing else is lacking. There remains nothing else for a person to receive that he doesn't already have, except for allowing their individual awareness to awaken to these truths.

You may not be able to clearly see all the reality of what Father has given, but you can patiently and contently expect Life and Life more abundantly to be your moment-by-moment experience. In the same way, also, our Holy Breath teaches us. IT helps with our inability to understand. Any hindrance comes from the habits we have developed over time, habits depending on the information we receive from our sensory realm. We must allow our Holy Breath to define what we see, hear, smell, taste, and feel. Without Spiritual understanding, we do not know how to agree with the Truth of who we are. Apart from listening to the Voice of our Holy Spirit within, we cannot properly see these things. The Voice of our Holy Breath is constantly beseeching us with the Words of Holy Breath, which are not understood by carnally minded people.

Furthermore, one who seeks, ascertains, and desires to know those things, of which our Holy Breath speaks, is able to understand correctly, become aware of, learn, and speak of those things which come from our Divine Mind. It is the purpose of our Father for us to know these things. Implore the Saints to passionately seek after, ascertain, and desire to know the one and only true Father, our Father. The whole of the Living inspired by Father's Word will work out Father's good purpose in them, according to what Jesus spoke while he ministered in this part of the world, and revealed to all who would listen with spiritual intelligence.

Our Father knew mankind in eternity and from the foundation of the world. Father declared, decreed, and determined that mankind Exists as the perfect resemblance or image of Father. All Father placed in us continues to exist eternally, just like it all existed in Jesus; we exist in oneness, age after age, eternally, world without end.

Therefore, we pre-existed in our eternal life; we also were declared to be Father's Sons and Daughters from the foundation. Father rendered us holy, pure, innocent, and right-wise. We are righteous in eternity, without beginning and without end. Since, from eternity, Father made us holy, pure, innocent, and right-wise, Father esteems us as the embodiment and image of Holy Breath. We radiate the image of our Papa, our Supreme Father. He admires us as a parent who would admire their child when it is born.

What, then, is left to say? We conclude that our Supreme Divine Father is our eternal Papa, and Papa is 100% for us and not against us. How can any act, whether we do it or someone else, conquer us in any way? Jesus revealed himself as a Son and, without a doubt, willingly submitted to the cruelty of the Pharisees and Sadducees' societal judgment. Our Holy Breath was in Jesus, revealing Father's Eternal Love and our eternal oneness with Father and everyone else. Our Supreme Papa showed our Holy Breath to us in Jesus. Now everything which we eternally possessed, was again brought to light.

What person or what action can question, bring to account, or lay any charge to our Papas' favorite people (chosen people, all people), who was chosen from the foundation, from eternity, world without end, from everlasting to everlasting? "Do you not know; Papa is particularly fond of you?" [Paul Young – The Shack]

If we know and understand this truth, what grounds can anyone provide to condemn us? In Jesus' crucifixion, death, and burial, he experienced societal judgment; he absorbed the Great Lie. In his resurrection, he REVEALED the Greater truth! This Greater truth is the final authority. Jesus spoke of these things in his time with all of you. He revealed how the law hindered man. In His passion on the Cross, He destroyed the law system of blood sacrifices. In His resurrection, He revealed Father's Love. Those truths are dominant. They are the final authority. So be it!

What person or deed could ever have the ability to separate or put asunder this marvelous love that our Wonderful, Great, and Marvelous Father has for us all.

Jesus revealed this love that Father had for all humanity? Can pressure from the world systems separate anyone from this wondrous love? No! Dis-tress? No! Maltreatment from those who resist the Truth? No! Irrational fear? No! A strong sense of lack? No! Erroneously believing yourself to be a mere human? No! Life-threatening danger? No! The expectation of a religiously imposed punishment? No!

My mandate, mission, and ministry are engraved in my whole being for your sake. My fellow ministers and I offer our lives to you daily. Because of our mandate, we are accounted as non-resisting fodder for the butchery of those mindful of the Mosaic Law. Nevertheless, in all this distress, maltreatment, and life threats, these things and more from those who do them are subdued and powerless because of our victory over them, revealed by Jesus' living mandate, mission, and ministry. Father is the one who eternally loved us. Jesus was victorious in what he was mandated to do; likewise, we are victorious we are mandated to do.

I agree and am persuaded by the truths Jesus revealed. Nothing can divide us from Father. Living as dead, having no awareness of our oneness with our Father doesn't divide us. Neither does living as alive, understanding our oneness with our Father. Teachers of the knowledge of good and evil, religious systems, or earthly rulers can't divide us. Nothing we know now or shall know in the future can separate us. No carnal power can separate us from Him.

No supposed higher knowledge apart from Father, no carnal mystery, nor any other human-made ordinance, decree, or declaration shall be able to place any division between Father and us. None of these things can separate us from Father's eternal love and our eternal Contact with our Papa Father, which Je-sus revealed in his resurrection. You can live your life based on these facts!

**Do you believe me when I tell you that you are HOLY, always have been holy, and always will be holy?**

As most of you know, my car tag states, "URHOLY." I enjoy watching people look over their steering wheel to see the tag, and I surely would like to hear their thoughts. Maybe they are thinking, "Who me," "you don't know what I've done," or "that's not what my Pastor says," or even, "The Bible does not say that." I'm sure that some will say, "Amen," and most of them are not "Church goers."

I was talking to Kay Fairchild concerning Jesus' language he spoke. We know he was of the Hebrew lineage and grew up in Jerusalem, so he spoke Hebrew and Aramaic languages. The original text or writings of others either was in Hebrew or Aramaic. When the books of the Bible were penned, the Old Outlook and Perception books were written in Hebrew, and the New Outlook and Perception books were pinned in Greek. Yes, some translations are pinned in the Aramaic language. However, today's bibles were translated from Hebrew and Greek to Latin, then to German, and then to English.

As of September 2020, the entire Bible has been translated into 704 languages, the New Testament has been translated into an additional 1,551 languages, and Bible portions or stories into 1,160 other languages.

Religious traditions state the "original Bible" was the Geneva translation, the primary Bible of 16th-century English Protestantism and used by William Shakespeare, Oliver Cromwell, John Knox, John Donne, and others. It was one of the Bibles taken to America on the Mayflower. Then the Catholic Religion got hold of it, and over 30,000 changes were made. More than 5,000 represent differences between the Greek text used for the Revised Version and that used as the Catholic religion's basis, the authorized King James Version.

With all those translations and over 30,000 changes, and probably more, there is a real need to study the Scripture with the view of our single eye (Divine Mind) to discover the not-concealed meaning of Scripture (the Word). Jesus said the Truth (not-concealed) Word will enable you to experience eternal freedom.

So, that's why I listen to Father as I translate Scripture from Greek and Hebrew to unveil what has been placed on the words in the Bible. Also, that is why I decree and declare that you are Holy, always have been Holy, and eternally will be Holy.

The Apostle Matthew recorded in the 22nd chapter of his historical story of Jesus and the goings-on in his day, "For many are called, but few are chosen." Remember that it is a version (English) of a version (German), of a Version (Latin), of a Version (Greek and Aramaic). I'm sure there were more versions before.

So, as I translated what Matthew wrote from Greek, I found a very different statement Jesus said: "All are Holy, but few chose to live as Holy."

What does it mean to be "holy?" The word "holy" is mentioned 744 times in the KJV of the Bible. The English word "holy" is first used in Exodus 3:5, and the Hebrew word qodesh (ko'-desh) means a sacred place or thing, including a person. Qodesh comes from the word Qadesh (kaw-dashe'), representing a scared person. You can also find another meaning for Qadesh, as a sanctuary. Next, we find the first mention of the English word "holy" in Matthews book, chapter 1, hagios (hag'-ee-os), which is from Hagos – sacred, pure, consecrated and as used in the KJV Saint, as a noun (person, place or thing) being sacred, including Messengers – Holy. In the Apostle Paul's book to the Hebrews, we find another Greek meaning of the English word "holy," which is hosios (hos'-ee-os), meaning right, divine character, pure – a sacred thing or person.

So, if "All are Holy, but few chose to live as Holy," why do they not choose to live as they are? I believe it is because most people in what we call "the Church," and almost all who are "out of the Church," were never told they were Holy and explained why. I have met many people who do not attend religious organizations who tell me they always knew they were Holy. I ask them how they know, and they almost always say, "God told me." Or even my Mother or Father told me I am Holy.

After the Apostle Paul presented his first few letters to the community of believers in Rome, he said, "Now, present yourself a living sacrifice, HOLY, acceptable to Father, which is your spiritual service." (Be who you BE – Holy, upright and pure) RERichmond Tree of Life Bible Translations

At the close of the Epistle of Romans, Paul sends his final greetings to the brothers and sisters who served in ministry. One was Aristobulus, who had a large household in Rome. The Greek meaning of Aristobulus is best deliberating, best advising, best counsel, and supreme deliberation (with one's self). We are holy, and we have within our entire being a Holy Mind, which we call, The Divine Mind, the Mind of Contact, or our Holy Breath. The Holy Breath of Father in and as us is not confined to one place in man but is active throughout our whole consciousness – everywhere present. The ideas and the inspiration of our Holy Breath (Spirit) are received by and abide by the understanding faculty, which is our Divine Mind.

The Hebrew word ark means a holy abode, a sanctuary, or a tabernacle. A treasury, and a BODY OF LIGHT.

You should be aware that Noah's ark figuratively pictures the spiritual part of oneself, built amid the flood of error. One makes one's ark on the scientific understanding of the wisdom, presence, and power of Father / Divine Mind / Source. The ark is built upon the affirmations of what one is in and as Holy Breath – Sons and Daughters of the eternal Father.

The Ark of the Covenant, a sacred ark, a holy thing, or an Ark (*presence of Father*) of the testimony, represents the original spark of divinity in man's being. It is a covenant, or agreement, of the Father with all Sons and Daughters that they have all the Father has. "All things whatsoever the Father hath are mine (and yours too) (John 16:15).

This original spiritual spark is sacred and holy because its development depends on man's immortality. It is represented as occupying the holiest place in the temple and as being protected and cared for with great devotion. All that man is has been brought forth from this central spark, yet the sense-conscious man often neglects it and ignores its existence. The attention is taken up with the things of sense to the exclusion of Spiritual things and understanding.

In individual consciousness, the spiritual forces are scattered when the ark of the covenant is removed from the heart center (city of Jerusalem). Because of the need for a substantial basis from which to operate, no definite spiritual unfoldment can take place. It was, therefore, necessary to establish this holy meeting place, as David (love) well knew (II Sam. 6:1-19). After David had fully learned that working with divine law always makes room for Truth Life and that disobedience is the cause of destruction, he brought the Ark of the Covenant back to its proper place in Jerusalem. Its presence there ensured the Israelites peace, harmony, and spiritual progress that they had not known during the absence of the Ark.

It is vital that being Holy, upright, and pure be part of our daily awareness and no longer ignored by what one sees in sensory awareness. We are Father's dwelling place, a Holy and Sacred sanctuary, and also in contact with Father / Divine Mind / Source, wherein a person becomes fully aware they are one with Father's pure Being. Our true selves will never be born in and upon us until we learn to turn within to our Holy Breath / Divine Mind / Father for light, guidance, and overcoming spiritual power. We are light healers – we heal people with the light of the Living Word; not just physical healing, but we heal peoples' conscious awareness. John wrote in his letter that we are the world's light; he said, "Now the true light shines." That's us. Yes, Jesus was a light of the world, but his intention was to revive man's fire so that they would be the light they were born to be.

To be Holy is to be in your awareness, Spiritual whole, and unimpaired innocence. (Webster Dictionary) Holiness is wholeness in Holy Breath, in your entire being. In this perfect conscious awareness, one is aware of the all-encompassing glory of Father in them as them.

We are "holy ground," which is a substance in its spiritual wholeness; that is, the idea of substance in the Divine Mind. When one approaches this, she or he must remove from understanding all limited thoughts of the Father – "put the shoes off your feet." Remove yourself from your old walk of life, and get back to walking with Father "in the cool of the day" – ruwach – Spirit / Holy Breath.

You were born as the Holy Temple, the Dwelling Place of Father – you are a spiritual body and soul, and you have contact with Father / Divine Mind / Holy Breath / Source, and you lack nothing.

**My meditation over the last few days; the subject of the need for all of us to EVOLVE in our knowledge and understanding. I am very aware that many of you are**

**evolving; however, millions of "Believers" desperately need to grow in spiritual understanding and knowledge.**

Did you know that what we call "Western Evangelical Christianity" has not EVOLVED in knowledge and understanding since its inception? Yet Science has EVOLVED considerably. Have you ever thought about that? Do you wonder why? Would you go to a Doctor that was educated 30 years ago or further back and never EVOLVED in his or her knowledge and understanding.

As a child, I grew up in several different Church religions; one thing each one taught me was not to believe in the science of evolution. The Britannica states "evolution," which is that biological evolution is the process of change and diversification of living things over time, and it affects ALL lives.

I'm afraid I have to disagree with Darwin's theory, but I believe that all life has evolved during what we call "time." However, more than just physical evolution, there has been an evolution of knowledge and understanding in all the sciences of the world.

The spiritual understanding of Eden is that it represents a region in which are provided all early stages of development of knowledge and ideas from the Father for the production of all beauty on this planet, including mankind. Eden allegorically represents the elemental Spiritual life and DIVINE intelligence placed at the disposal of mankind, and through which he or she is to EVOLVE in awareness as a Living Soul.

The human body comprises the Garden of Eden. When a man develops and EVOLVES in spiritual insight, thought, word, and act and voluntarily operates according to their Divine Mind and Divine Law of Life. Rulership, authority, and dominion become his or hers. The kingdom of God is within every part of your being, and when that Kingdom is involved in your conscious awareness, your Divine Mind / Father / Source EVOLVES through you. You experience a spiritual evolution that energizes your being.

Mankind is a creature of free will, yet in a larger sense, they are a Son or Daughter of Father / Source, made in the image and likeness of Father, and are destined to EVOLVE, express, and demonstrate the spiritual perfection they have and are. In all the universe, including man, there is a balancing power of perfection, which causes a readjustment or healing of awareness, to allow a perfect evolution to greater heights of consciousness and the ability to do the more significant things Jesus, the Great Comforter Messenger said we could. Many people are doing the "greater things" now; it is the ability to teach and explain the Living Word of Truth that Jesus desired to teach those around him in Jerusalem.

We find this set forth very clearly in Bible history and the symbolism of each story. The man wandered away from spiritually evolving to living a false life of limitation.

The Western Christian Evangelical systems have not allowed themselves or their followers to EVOLVE spiritually or even in their conscious awareness. The majority of so-called "Leaders" in those systems have not grown one bit more than what they learned at their Seminary schools or from the Church they attended in their youth. The truth of that statement is very easily seen in the followers of their over 44,000 "Christian" denominations. You can talk with followers from every age, and very few have EVOLVED in an understanding of who Father is or who they are. They still believe and follow what they were told 80 or 90 years ago.

Why is it that in religiosity, there needs to be more evolution of what the people know, and yet, in all other systems, the science of their system excels almost yearly, if not daily? And yet, in the Church world, people hear the same teachings and sermons year after year and do not change one bit in understanding. Some of my past teachers I studied under 20 or more years ago still teach almost word for word what they taught then. Why? Because they are not spiritually evolving in their conscious awareness.

I desire to live a life of Evolution – Growth, Advancement, Development, and daily progress in my understanding of the Living Word, who and what our Source Father is, and know myself and you as Father knows us; perfect, enough,, and altogether lovely.

Are you happy where you are or are you one who desires to ever evolve in your conscious awareness to experience the perfect being you are? Your growth in Contact with Father / Divine Mind will accelerate significantly as you come into the ideal knowledge of the not-concealed Word that causes you to experience eternal freedom. You will think and act consciously, in perfect harmony with the Divine Mind / Father / Source / Chi.

Involution is another word for involvement. Involving with the Living Word and your Divine Mind always precedes evolution, an unfolding of all you are and were from the foundation. That applied in their Divine Mind evolves to show forth the glory they already have, being the exact image of Father. Everything is present in the evolution of the Soul. The moment a person walked into a place of supposed Spiritual learning, that day should have been a day of a New Beginning, but not the new beginning religiosity taught them was not what they needed.

The numerical number eight appears numerous times in the Bible. Eight is the biblical number for a New Beginning or a New order of things. Eight is a symbol of Infinity, which has no beginning or end. The movement of the hand in writing, the number eight, is a rhythmic repetition that suggests action and reaction, involution and evolution. Eight also means splendor, fullness, greatness, immensity, and infinity.

Spiritually, this means when you become aware that the "I Exist" in you is Father, pure Being, Life, and Awareness. As you tune in with the Infinite, knowing that the Life-Principle is the Father of all and that all people are your brother and sisters, you will sense your oneness with all life and with all people throughout the world. As you claim that which is true of Father is also true of you, you will go from glory to glory and from octave to octave, symbolized by the numeral eight, which has no beginning or end. Eight means you are moving onward, upward, and Godward. The moment you realize you are the tabernacle of the Living Father and when you divest yourself of your name, nationality, social status, and all things having a bearing on your personality, you realize you are unveiling the God Presence, which is the eighth day, or eighth hour, or eighth Son or Daughter – one moving upward, forward and Godward.

So, is spiritual evolution vital to us, the world, and its inhabitants? Yes, it is. Evolving and evolution is the development achieved while working under spiritual law and life. It results from the development of Father's ideas in your Divine Mind. What we project in our lives is the result of the evolution of our consciousness, and this consciousness is the result of seed ideas sown in one's awareness. In the beginning, Father implanted a perfect word and involved this seed word into each person, and it continues at the conception of every child born of a woman. Evolution is the unfolding in the consciousness of that which Father involved in man in the beginning.

Spiritual evolution is the unfolding of the Holy Breath of the Father, in us, into expression. The Son or Daughter of Father being the evolution in mankind is plainly taught in the New Outlook and Perception Books as the supreme attainment of every man. "For the earnest expectation of the creation waiteth for the revealing of the sons of God"

(Rom. 8:19). As the reality of the original formation of people evolves in our awareness, we come to clearly see what Father has conferred upon us. We fully live as the Sons and Daughters of Father that we presently are.

The meaning of Life is to Evolve Spiritually to who you presently are.

**Did you know Jesus was a healer?**

I'm sure you are saying, "Yes!" And yes because you've read of the many physical and mental healings he performed. However, his being a healer was not to heal physical and mental recuperation. He was in the cities to heal people of their mistaken identity and false perception of who and what Father, our Source, really is. He was and is a spiritual healer; yes, I believe he is still on Earth. If you saw him, you would not know who he was.

We all came here to do the same thing; to heal the people in our world of their false perceptions and who they were told they were from birth.

So, Jesus' desire and mandate was to be the spiritual healer he was to all who came to him.

When Jesus sent his Disciples out to heal people, I believe they misunderstood Jesus' real intentions. However, they still ministered out of their awareness and brought physical healing to many. I think Jesus told them to heal people of their false perception of the Father and who they were created to be.

In my many ministry years, I've often wondered why I have not experienced praying over people for physical healing and seeing many results, not that I do not believe in physical healing. However, physical healing is temporal, and the need for recovery will return for the same or other situations. What people need is a healing that brings permanence of Life in every area of their Soul; that healing is a spiritual healing of the Truthful word brought to people that will wake them up spiritually and cause them to experience Life and Life more abundantly than we already possess.

My mission, mandate, and ministry are to remove false perceptions of people and their awareness and then plant many seeds of Truth in them.

In 1988, I was teaching the book of Jeremiah, in the Adult Sunday School class, at Full Gospel Assembly. One night while studying Jeremiah, I asked Father why the Priest rejected Jeremiah and fought him. Father spoke to my thoughts and said, "I am going to make you like Jeremiah and will give you words to speak, and no matter how people respond, to continue speaking the words given to me." I have never stopped, and everything I heard from Father came to pass. Furthermore, Father spoke to my thoughts to re-read Jeremiah chapter 1, which would be my driving reminder anytime I felt great rejection from those who were grounded in religiosity. I am a Mystic and a Comforter Messenger who seeks and teaches Spiritual knowledge and understanding. I desire to always function as a spiritual healer with the words, actions, and love I pour out to all who hunger for more.

**4** Then the word of the LORD came unto me, saying,

**5** Before I formed thee in the belly I knew thee; and before thou camest forth out of the womb I sanctified thee, and I ordained thee a prophet unto the nations.

**6** Then said I, Ah, Lord GOD! behold, I cannot speak: for I am a child.

**7** But the LORD said unto me, Say not, I am a child: for thou shalt go to all that I shall send thee, and whatsoever I command thee thou shalt speak.

**8** Be not afraid of their faces: for I am with thee to deliver thee, saith the LORD.

**9** Then the LORD put forth his hand, and touched my mouth. And the LORD said unto me, Behold, I have put my words in thy mouth.

**10** See, I have this day set thee over the nations and over the kingdoms, to root out, and to pull down, and to destroy, and to throw down, to build, and to plant.

## Mystics – a Spiritual Seeker of Wisdom, Knowing, and Understanding.

Many "believers" seem to shy away from people who are mystics. They do not understand the meaning of the word. A "Mystic" is one who, when studying or even looking at the world and its inhabitants, looks below the surface level of what is seen with the body's eyeballs. Did you know your eyeballs do not "see" anything? They are transmitters of light to the brain, and then the brain forms the image. Sometimes the thoughts and beliefs in your brain twist and distort that which is transmitted.

Have you had anyone explain something to you, and then you said, "Oh, I see now?" You did not see anything; your ears heard words as waves, transmitted them to your brain, and formed thoughts or understanding you saw in your mind's eye.

Paul said to be carnally mindful is death (no intimacy with Father), but spiritually mindful, is life and perfection.

The words "mystic or mystical mean "Spiritual." A person who gleans by Spiritual understanding and knowledge is a mystic; they are not satisfied with what lies on the surface of a thing or matter. They even look through how a person presents themselves on the outside, actions or deeds, and see what lies within - Spirit - a Son or Daughter of the One God - Holy and Upright.

Proverbs 25:2 states, "It is the glory of God to conceal a thing: but the honor of kings is to search out a matter."

The Kings are Mystics who search out the matter; we are unsatisfied with the surface (carnal) level of understanding.

In the King James Version of the word, Job said, "Surely there is a vein for the silver, and a place for the gold where they fine it." Silver is the biblical metal for Redemption, and Gold is Divine Nature. The English word "fine" was translated from the Hebrew word "Zaqaq," (zaw-kak') extract, purify, and clarify; hence making it palatable or understandable.

My translation of Job 28:1 There exists a great fountain of Life-Force, within us, that reveals the awesomeness of Redemption and Righteousness, and the decree of our Divine Nature is clarified." RERichmond Tree of Life Bible Translations

The question for you is, Do you want to feed on carnally mindful teachers who teach the surface level of the word that has been prepared for hundreds of years and brought no real help to the earth, OR are you ready for the anointed Mystics to get you to the Truth that will make you free to live out of who you really are - a Supernatural Daughter or Son of the One and only Living Father/Source/God in you.

The Marriage Supper is dining on the Living Word, not the written word. The Living Word is a deep wellspring just below the surface word, which is the creative spiritual law-giving and revealing activity.

If you were taught that Father instructed Abraham to take Isaac up to a mountain and offer him a burnt offering to test his faith, you should read the following snippet from one of my documents.

OT:5930 'olah (o-law'); or 'owlah (o-law'); to ascend, be high, to mount. Feminine; active participle of OT:5927; to ascend step or (collectively, stairs, as ascending); KJV - ascent.
(Biblesoft's New Exhaustive Strong's Numbers and Concordance with Expanded Greek-Hebrew Dictionary. Copyright © 1994, 2003, 2006 Biblesoft, Inc. and International Bible Translators, Inc.)

Genesis 2:22 Abraham, take your beloved Son and ascend to the land of Moriah; go there with Isaac. I will tell you which mountain to ascend to. Father wanted Abraham and Isaac to come alone with Father in a mountain top (mountains are always a place of learning), so He could instruct them, that HE was not like the false gods and the religions they had embraced in the past, and he desired nor needed any sacrifices of appeasement.

Dr. Roy E. Richmond – Tree of Life Bible Translations
DrRoyERichmond.com YouTube channel – Dr. Roy E. Richmond

## Did you know you never had an "old man?"

The King James Version and other versions of the Bible, they used the phrase "old man" in Romans 6:6, Ephesians 4:22, and Colossians 3:9.
On each occasion, the Greek word is the NT: #3820 palaios (pal-ah-yos'), meaning antique and worn out. Now, many would say that is our "Old Man." Well, not necessarily.

In Romans 6:6, the Greek rendering is, "In this, be aware that the antique and worn out part of (not our) Adam (the first race of man) is crucified." We know Paul said, my ego died, being me, myself and I, as living in the sense of separateness from Father. So did Mankind die, or did an old, antique, worn-out awareness die?
Ephesians 4:22 Paul talks about the conversations from the old, worn-out awareness.

Colossians 3:9 Pual discusses putting off the deeds produced from an old worn-out awareness.

We were created Holy and Upright and always retained that position. Therefore, mankind never became an "old man." - it was man's low-lander awareness that was worn out and needed to be raised back up. The "Newness" of life never left mankind. Father continued to seek to clothe mankind in greater awareness, by sending Messengers of the Lord, Prophets, Jesus, and now many Comforter Messengers - Man never became Old in Father's view. Whose view are you going to believe?

Yes, we need to seek Divine wisdom, knowledge, and understanding. But is intuitive knowing, spiritual intuition; the Holy Voice (Breath) within as the source of our knowledge; mental action based on the Divine Mind (in Contact with Father) within. Wisdom includes righteous judgment, discrimination, intuition, and all the departments of the brain that come under the head of knowing."

This "knowing" capacity transcends intellectual knowledge. Spiritual discernment always places wisdom above the other faculties of consciousness, revealing that learning and intelligence are secondary to spiritual understanding. Wisdom and divine understanding; these attributes come from the Divine Mind or Holy Breath within us. The price we must pay for the conscious attainment of divine wisdom and knowledge is letting go of the Ego, with its limited beliefs.

Paul saw the Divine Mind waiting at the awareness of every soul when he wrote: "Awake, thou that sleepiest, and arise from the dead, and illuminate as one Spirit." (Eph. 5:14)." What he said died in him when Jesus died, was "I" being his ego (me, myself, and I). After believing and seeing what Jesus revealed in his earth walk and Passion work, he realized that the old ego mentality ceased to exist in him. The awakening Paul often talked about is that man is furnished with a permanent, inexhaustible source of life, love, wisdom, intelligence, power, strength, and every good that he can need or desire (endowed, given, bestowed). This source is Father Himself in mankind, who in the ideal Man, the Son, is the true self of everybody and expresses in and through each individual just to the extent that the individual gives their Holy Breath cooperation. We do not have a lower self; there is only one self, Son (no gender implied).

**Did you know  death results from living with the universal belief of good and bad, thus, living with carnal thoughts and in a carnal realm?**

Death also results from living with mistaken identity, trying to obey the many religious laws of doing to be, and not discerning one's Spirit within. Paul explained the reason for weakness, sickness, and physical death is that man does not understand they are Spirit; therefore, they do not live out of their Holy Spirit.

Death is not only physical death. However, if the cause is allowed to continue, it will end in physical death. Therein lies a great problem; for far too long, physical death has been the norm in man's mindset – we have believed it is inevitable and "no one can escape physical death." I chose to consider what the Apostle knew to be a fact – "This mortality (liable to die mentality) must put on immortality (unending existence mentality). [Second Corinthians 5:4]

The word 'mortality' is the NT #2349 thnetos (thnay-tos'; liable to die: A Liable to die mindset. 'Immortality' has three Greek meanings: Number one is NT: #861 aphthrsia (af-thar-see'-ah) unending existence. Number two is NT: #862; incorruptibility; genitive case endless existence, as the First. The third is NT: #110 athanasia (ath-an-as-ee'-ah), as the First Man - deathlessness.

Romans 8:6 "For to be carnally minded is death, but to be spiritually minded is life and peace." KJV

Romans 8:6-7 Tree of Life Bible Translation - 6 For someone to seek, be mindful and desire that which is external is to cut themselves off from that which is Spiritual. Moreover, being conscious of what is of our Holy Breath brings the realization of wholeness, Life, and Perfection. 7 If a person exercises their thoughts and desires for that which brings no Life, they put themselves in a position opposite of living as the embodiment of our Father Creator. The lustful desire for that which is not Spirit is diametrical, opposed to the prescription of living out of our Holy Spirit.

"The sense of the flesh realm, which is sense and reason, without leaning to our Holy Spirit (mind of Christ), is death; the death that comprises all miseries arising from the consequences of living as a man whose breath is in his or her nostrils. But the mind of the Spirit is life [soul] and peace, both now and forever."

**Did you know - The Law did not come from Father but from an angry Moses.**

Moses was angry with the children of Israel. All through the journey to the Promised Land, they murmured and cried for meat, cried to return to Egypt, and fought against his leadership. Like many religious leaders, he became angry with Father's people and devised rules, regulations, and laws to control them. It never works because laws do not change a person's behavior, character, and nature. Nevertheless, the children of Israel and all future generations believed the Law came from Father God. They, and many today, continue to try to obey "do to be" Laws, and in so doing, they bring a curse upon themselves. The first proof of this statement is from the Apostle John, who correctly understood Father's love.

"For the law by Moses was given; grace and truth revealed by Jesus Christ." Therefore, the Law was given by Moses, not our Papa Father.

So, they kept struggling to obey the law to become something they already were. In doing that, they brought a sense of guilt and self-condemnation into their lives, which created what Moses called their curse – weakness, sickness, and death of the body. By faith, put down your "do to be" law, and stand upright and be who you be – righteous, holy, pure, as Son and Daughter of God.

A long time ago, in a place far, far away, lived two women, one old and one relatively young. Both ladies were traveling through a blazing desert with hot rocks and sand on a mission. The elder woman was going home, and the young lady was determined to become a refuge in the elders' home. The elder woman went by the name Nahomi; she had lost everything; her husband, her children, and her financial support. The younger was named Ruth; she was a Moabite. Ruth was married to a son that died. They both returned to Bethlehem, the home of Nahomi, totally bankrupt; they both were faced with living a mundane and ordinary life, with no hope of finances or food being provided.

Ruth goes into the field to gather the leftover seed because that is what ordinary people were allowed to do in those days. Nahomi got so down that she changed her name to Marah, meaning bitter. She said my life is turning to bitterness – I lost everything. Boaz shows up – and Ruth marries him. Forty years from then, Nahomi's great-great-grandchild was called Jessi, and one of his sons was David, who became King of Israel. King David's future generation produced a child named Jesus.

Are you one who thinks your life is mundane and boring, never to be famous or do anything significant in the world? How would you live your life, knowing that in generations after your body ceased to be able to hold you, there would be a seed born that would change the entire world, come up with a cure for cancer, or become a great scientist in another area?

You might think your life means nothing and is boring, and yet, a Great Comforter Messenger can come through your seed if you faithfully tend your life, who will bring a great Light to the world. Do not cut off your seed by not living fully - live your life in all joy. At your inception, it was Father's life that placed the work in you.

The Ark of the eternal Covenant was taken by the Philistines, who symbolize dust-dwellers or carnally mindful people. The Ark of the Covenant, sacred Ark, or Ark of the testimony, represents the original spark of Divinity in man's being. It is a covenant or an agreement of the Father with all Sons and Daughters that they possess all that the Father is and has. We can say, like Jesus, "All things whatsoever the Father has are mine." [John 16:15]

This original spiritual spark is a very sacred, holy thing. The development of this spark results in man's awareness of his immortality. It is represented as occupying the holiest place in the Temple and is protected and cared for with great devotion.

All that man is has been brought forth from this Central Holy Spark, yet the sense-conscious man is often unaware of its existence. Their attention is consumed with sensual desires to the exclusion of Holy Breath.

In individual consciousness, the spiritual forces are scattered when the Ark of the covenant is removed from the heart center (city of Jerusalem). Because of the need for a substantial basis from which to operate, no spiritual unfoldment can take place. Establishing this holy meeting place was necessary, as David (love) well knew. (II Sam. 6:1-19)

David learned that working with Divine spiritual law always brings good. From his own experience, he also knew that not listening to Father with intelligence is the cause of destruction, which are a consequence of his choices.

David returned the Ark of the Covenant to its proper place in Jerusalem. Its presence brought the Israelites a measure of peace and harmony. Though their experience of peace was minimal, it was spiritual progress they had yet to learn when the Ark was absent.

**Be calm, quiet and know…**

It is a rare person that spends any quality time in silence. The world is built around satisfying the senses with sensual pleasures and influences. In fact, very few there are who can actually silence their thoughts. And yet, Scripture exhorts us, "To be still and know." One of the English words, "Still," comes from the Hebrew word "chashah (khaw-shaw'), meaning to hush and keep silent.

Psalm 4:4 gives instruction, "To stand in awe, and quit living with a mistaken identity syndrome (sin): stay in contact with Father while you rest; hush and be quiet – listen to Father's voice of love." Psalm 45:10 says, "Hush and be quiet, and intimately know that I Exist as your Father: I Exist in all people of the earth, and I Exist in all the earth." Psalm 84:4, "Happy and well off are they who comfortably EXIST as my Holy Temple: they in quietness and silence reveal My nature in them." RERichmond Tree of Life Bible

In Mark 4:39, we find that Jesus was asleep in a boat with his disciples, and a great storm was raging, and they ran to get Jesus, saying do you not care if we perish? He got up and went to the front of the boat, forbade the harsh wind, and said to the storm, Perfection from you, hush and be quiet," The clouds and rain returned to their perfect intention – to gently water the earth.

The disciples were afraid, even when Jesus was in their boat with them.

Guess who is in your boat? The Father of all Creation, hush and be quiet - and speak perfection and peace over the world softly.

## Our Divine Mind

Many people talk about what they must do in the "Church." They say we must rise, rule, reign, and we must do this and that. Their focus is all about do, do, do. We must know and become aware that the Divine mind is inside us. Our Divine Mind will rule and reign naturally when we realize and embrace this truth.

This then causes one to seek to know Father more intimately and the Great Oneness Operation from the foundation. Then he or she can tell the Truthful Story with no mixture. The "Greater is your Holy Breath that is within you" must come forth. The inner man is the Father's life. The same Life Jesus possesses is the same life-giving force in all Sons and Daughters. We all have the same Divine Mind Jesus lived (lives) out of – but we need to learn to possess IT and live out of it just as Jesus revealed. When we possess Father's Mind within, we will do the "greater works" Jesus spoke of.

**When studying Scripture, we must allow Father to open our single eye (spiritual eye or third eye), so we can see spiritually, not carnally.**

We must look below a surface-level understanding of scripture and discover the depth of the riches, both of the wisdom and knowledge of our Father. I am overwhelmed and apprehended by the depth of the riches, both of the wisdom and knowledge of our Father. We can discover wisdom and knowledge by listening to the Voice of our Holy Breath. Wisdom and knowledge are not fully searched for or tracked by most people. Most people have never really known our Father, but they can.

**I hope you know by now that "the power of God" is within you.**

Solomon wrote in the book of Wisdom, "For wisdom is more moving than any motions; She passeth and goeth through all things because of pureness. For She is the Breath of the POWER OF GOD, and a pure influence flowing from the glory of the Almighty; therefore, can no defiled thing fall into Her. For She is the brightness of the everlasting, the unspotted mirror (image) of the power of God, and the image of his goodness. And being but one, She can do all things: and remaining in herself, She maketh all things fresh: and in all ages She is active Souls as the creative spiritual law giving and revealing activity. She maketh them Prophets and Messengers of Truth."

There are in the world today (and past) men and women who have followed the teaching of Jesus and Paul and discovered in their bodies a super-energy or Life that not only permeates the physical structure but envelops it in a luminous aura that can be and is felt by both themselves and others. Father reveals that spiritual thinking breaks open the physical cells and atoms and releases life initially from Divine Mind. Jesus carried this process so far that His whole body was transformed and became a conscious part of the Father's life and intelligence.

I wish this for you. We must keep our awareness of spiritual knowledge and the understanding that comes to all who seek Truth.

If you want to experience infinite spiritual enlightenment, you need to realize that soon you will rise to a level of awareness, that if you cross over, you never can go back.

**Scripture reveals that "God is Spirit."**

The word "spirit" was wrongly used when they translated ruwach. Ruwach is the Hebrew number 7307, and it means Breath or Breathe. We breathe in the Living Word of our Creator, and then our Breath carries it out into our world and our entire being. Ruwach can also mean "to make a quick understanding." So, as you read our books, you will see various descriptions of our Creator as "God, Father, He, and Him." We use those pronouns to help people gain a "quick understanding." We use these names because most people were taught that Father is a physical person with the gender male. Our Source, Father, Breath, and Creator, meets us where we are in our awareness. Some might need a male to be a version of Father; others might need a female to be a version of Father, then there are those who currently, in their awareness, see Holy Breath as God. The truth is, our Creator meets you where you are, in your awareness.

Interestingly, the word "air" in scripture denotes the deific breath of God. It symbolizes a purifying, vitalizing power that revives and keeps life. The term "deific" means making divine or exalting to the position of a God – hence God-like – Divine. As we Breathe in the Truthful Living Word, we awaken more and more to our God-likeness, Divine Character, and Nature. When any person is inspired by that which is true and Divine, they breathe "into their nostrils the breath of life." Genesis 2:7, "…and breathed in their nostrils the breath of life, and MAN (no gender implied) became a living soul."

Man is Holy Breath (Spirit), absolute and unconditioned. Mankind is to form a consciousness into which he or she breathes (in and out) the breath of life; this, in its perfect expression, is the "Son of man," an expression of the divine idea. Mankind is all of what we term Soul. We are continually at work in our teaching to breathe the breath of life into our follower's nostrils, inspiring them with the accurate idea of life in all its unlimited fullness. We can lift up all who will "come and see" or "come and hear" by infusing these magnificent thoughts and truths into them, and in no other way. Our Holy Breath is the silent movement of our Creator within man. There is Holy Breath in every person ever born. Job said, as recorded in Job 33:3, "The Breath of God hath made me, and the Breath of the Almighty hath given me LIFE." You can say the same thing about yourself.

Breathing is the symbol of inspiration. Jesus breathed on his Apostles and said to them, Receive ye the Holy Ghost." The word "receive, was wrongly translated from the NT:2983 word lambano. Lambano means to take or get hold of. So, the Apostles already possessed Holy Breath; they only needed to be educated that they were and possessed Holy Breath, and they needed to take or get hold of IT to do the work of ministry they were set apart to do. The "breath of God," which became the soul of the man manifestation, includes all emotions and energies (deific) that move in and through the body, and it is always designated as feminine. Psyche is the name of that subtle essence (air) that flows in and out of the great heart center called in physiology, the cardiac plexus.

There was a river in Eden named Gihon. Gihon is a Hebrew word that determines impulse, formative movement, a bursting forth, rapid stream. Gihon represents the deific breath of the Father, inspiring mankind and purifying their consciousness. The Holy Breath of the Father infuses us, endowing us with super light and life.

Jerah was a descendant of Shem and the founder of an Arabian tribe (Gen. 10:26). His name in Hebrew means radiating brother; he will breathe and become inspired. We pray that what you learn from our teachings will do exactly that to you; you will become radiated and breathe in and out the Living Word to your world.

There are many names and titles in Scripture that carry the same meanings; place of fragrance; his sweet breath' his life; is animated; living; breathing; soul; spirit; he will become inspired, and much more.

When our awareness finds balance in Truth, all lesser ideas die or disappear through transfiguration. Even the ideas that seem to contain the "breath of the spirit of life" are lost in the fuller realization of the Father as the only presence and power.

When mankind lets go of the false sense of things and discerns Father as the one source of all good, they rest in spiritual consciousness with pure ideas of Being.

**From my translations:**

Ephesians 4:1:6 says, "From this view, vision, and love of our Father I possess, I invite and invoke you to embrace the realization I am apprehended with for yourselves; appropriately tread about your life calling, which you are worthy of. 2 with all humbleness of mind and mildness, with patience, hold up one another, in a relationship of rest and love without a cause. 3 With eagerness, guard everyone's Oneness of Holy Breath, at rest and in the control of perfection and peace, 4 in one body and one Holy Breath, as even you are called, in a relation of rest, one expectation and confidence of your invitation, 5 that there is only One Source (Father), and one faith to put your faith in, and that is Fathers' faith, and one immersion of awareness of being One with and as Father; 6 in the one

Supreme Divinity, the Father of all, Who is above all wrongly perceived ideas of Father (false gods – and false versions of Father), the One who is the Source of all, and in all." RERichmond Tree of Life Bible Translations

The original meaning of the word "still," used in "still small voice" and also in "Be still and know, is "Calm and quiet." Father's Voice is always calm and quiet. That negates the thought that Father could ever be angry with you; even when He spoke from a mountaintop to Moses, He did not speak to Moses' thoughts with anger.

When we converse with Father, it should always be from a quiet and calm position, just as Father converses with us.

Father was and continues to be presented as angry by people who get their understanding from embracing the teachings of religiosity; don't let them interpenetrate your awareness.

**At four am, before my open heart surgery (March 1st, 2022), I heard Father speak Psalm 23 to my thoughts. I**

**had no idea how tough the surgery would be or that I would die the next day and the following day.**

**Mediate on this often:**

These are the exact words I heard.

"The Father eternally tends to me; I have no lack. My home and body are full of life, as a green pasture. The Living Water of the Word* fills me to overflowing. He sustains my soul, being the cause of me eternally being upright and in all peace, perfection, and Joy. Even though all around me, there is a sense of death in this world, I will not fear anything that seems to be bad. For you, Father, are with and in me always, for Your Living Word* and guidance bring great comfort to me, and I feel Your warm breath surrounding me."

I was being prepared for the next eight days in intensive care.

*"Word" - the creative spiritual law-giving and revealing activity.

During the Civil War in the USA, Doctors were sent to cities close to the battlefields and also out in the area where the fighting occurred. They amputated limbs and performed various other surgeries. One can imagine how much blood got on their clothing and hands. They wore the blood on their clothing like a badge of courage and did minimal cleaning between their patients. They also assisted women in giving birth in the city's around them after caring for the wounded soldiers.

The doctors discovered many of the mothers ended up dying a week or so after the babies were born.
One Doctor felt they were doing something wrong, and he began to study the blood of the deceased and living mothers. He discovered something no other Doctor had discovered yet: germs.

He was so excited at his discovery. He felt they were spread from the blood and other bodily fluids that the Doctors carried on them because they did not wash their hands very well or change their garments before they went to their next patient, including the mothers. He wanted to tell everyone what he had learned.

So, this Doctor began to declare what he had learned and told the other Doctors they needed to change their garments after each surgery and wash their arms and hands thoroughly. With that, the Doctors began to mock him and speak ill of him. They told other Doctors not to listen to him; after all, no one in the medical field had ever heard of such a thing as "germs." The attack on this Doctor became so vicious that they drove him insane, and he ended up in an institution.

In 1869, only four years after the conclusion of the Civil War, Scottish physician Dr. Joseph Lister published his paper proposing the first truly popular modern germ theory. Other well-known Doctors followed his study; they discovered the other Doctor was correct. Germs were the problem; they were spread by Doctors who did not change their garments or wash their hands thoroughly.

This story can be told of any forerunner who discovers greater truths concerning knowledge and wisdom.

Father inspired Jeremiah to write the following to Israel: Jeremiah 3:15 And I will give you pastors according to my awareness, which shall feed you with knowledge and understanding. KJV

Why do people turn against those who study, teach and share more excellent knowledge and understanding that conforms with Father's heart (awareness)? I think it might be pride and insecurity, and because of that, they spread "germs of division."

Speaking out against someone who teaches what you still need to understand is not wise. Just because you do not understand something, or it is not being taught in your circle of teachers, does not mean it is wrong; your perception might be off. Contacting that teacher and saying, "I do not understand what you are sharing would be wiser. Would you please explain this more to me?"

It is possible to let go of the life that was inherited from the past, to live the One who is waiting to come forth from our inner being. The death that was passed on does not have to be received. Where did that ego -(me, myself and I) come from? We were not born with it; it was taught and acquired from others. Let it go.

**The Wonders of our Body.**

The following, is some of what I have gleaned from several Ancient writings I study, all of which discuss Mankind as stated in the following Psalm:

Psalms 139:13-14
13 For thou hast possessed my reins: thou hast covered me in my mother's womb. 14 I will praise thee; for I am fearfully and wonderfully made: marvelous are thy works; and my soul knoweth right well.
KJV

When I look at the members of my body, I am always amazed at the wonders of its systems and how they give life, movement, and action to the whole. In the many bible translations, we, as a group, are often given the title of "The Church." In translating the word "church" from the original Greek, we find the word "ekklesia" (ek-klah-see'ah), which is used in many writings. However, searching the root word, I found "ek," which denotes origin, as in the point whence action or motion proceeds. Without a doubt, throughout history, the human race has been asleep, dreaming that property, money, and power are the true wealth of a nation. I enjoy watching movies from the days of Kings, Queens, Knights, and many other characters during that age. They exemplify that dream of property, money, and power as their wealth while sacrificing men, women, and children to gain what they desire. The result is seen in the uneasiness of life that prevails in every age, every nation, and every country.

I read many writings of authors who lived in the fourteen hundreds, and forward and those who wrote during what we call "biblical times." Without exception, every one of the writers felt in their day, humanity was waking up, slowly but surely, and discovering that Mankind, itself, is the most precious thing on earth. However, the majority were not waking up. Only a few will wake up to who they indeed are and to the knowledge of our Source Father. Thus, if you are one, it is essential to awaken and be a shining beckon to your world.

I believe there will be an age where the masses will awaken and pray it will be in our day. But, I will not say the day of the masses' awakening is "our day." We are forerunners who are laying down a solid foundation of Truth that we are available when the masses seek what their soul really desires.

In my early years of study, I read many commentaries and many translations of bibles. All of them implied that we are a race of imperfect people who need saving from "God" and need laws to follow, to aline us with their many religious laws. They are wrong; every person born of a woman is perfect in Father's vision.

As King David knew and wrote, "Father covered us in our mother's womb, and we are reverentially and wonderfully made; Wonderful are your works."

As it is the carpenter's business to take the lumber which perfected as material and build the house, it is the legitimate work of the spiritual man to take the perfect material everywhere present and builds by the ideal law of chemistry and mathematics the perfected harmonious human being and with this material employ the same law to build up society collectively.

It is a well-known physiological fact that blood is the basic material of which the human body is continually built. As is the blood, so is the body; as is the body, so is the brain; as is the brain, so is the quality of thought. Scripture states, "As a man thinks in his awareness, so is he." We say, "As a man thinks in his awareness, so is his realization," or we can say, "As a man is built, so thinks he." Numerous times, the phrase "build-up" in used to build up the temple, the house, the wall of Jerusalem, the throne, and the city. All those items metaphorically speak of humanity. So, there must be a building up in ourselves; that place is our conscious awareness. We are rooted and built up in Father, established in Father's faith in us. The Apostle Peter wrote, we are lively stones, and are built up a spiritual house, and a holy priesthood.

According to the views of students of modern alchemy, the Bible – both the Old and the New Outlook books, are symbolical, parabolical, and allegorical. Each book is based primarily upon the very process of bodybuilding. The Word alchemy really means flesh-ology. Flesh-ology is drawn from chem, an ancient Egyptian word meaning flesh. The term "Egypt" also means flesh or anatomy.

Alchemy, in its broader scope, means the science of solar rays. Gold may be traced to the sun's rays. The Word gold means solar essence. Biblically, gold is the metal for Divine Nature. Also, as Kay Fairchild posted on my last FB teachings, "The ancients also believed that the word "gold," since it does not corrode, was a symbol of immortality and "silver" meant emotions yielded to Spirit—Or fully redeemed emotions (in a subjective sense).

These students of Alchemy say that the transmutation of gold does not mean the process of making gold but means the process of changing gold and solar rays into all materialized forms, vegetables, minerals, etc. These ancients studied the cycle of nature in her operations from the volatile to the fixed, the fluid to the solid, the essence to the substance, or abstract to the concrete, all of which may be summed up in the changing Spirit into the matter. Or we could say, "spirit slowed down the visibility."

In reality, the true alchemist did not try to do anything. He tried to search out nature's process so that he might comprehend the marvelous operations of our Source Father. Mankind's most significant problem is they always try to "do to be," not knowing what or who they were born to be.

To be sure, language was used, which seems symbolic and often contradictory, but it was neither intended nor so in reality. To our detriment, we read old writings, including our bibles, and take everything we read as literal rather than symbolic, parabolical, and metaphorical. We often speak in symbols. When someone does something silly to us, we say, "That is out of their minds." Of course, no one supposed the person to be out of their mind.

So, it is alchemy that the old and new Outlook books are a collection of alchemical and astrological writing that deals with the beautiful operation of the Spirit and the body so fearfully and wonderfully made. The same authority is given from the statements,

"Know not that your bodies are the temple of the Living God." And "Come unto me, all you labor and are heavy laden, and I will give you rest." Thus, by realizing that the body is really the Father's house, the temple of God, the Spirit secures peace and contentment or rest.

The human body comprises perfect principles, gases, minerals, molecules, or atoms. But these builders are flesh, and bones are only sometimes correctly adjusted. The planks or bricks used in building houses may be innocently diversified in arrangement and yet be the perfect material.

Solomon's Temple is an allegory of man's temple, the human Organism. The house is built, or always being made, without the sound of a saw or hammer.

We manifest in a house, church, or temple as I Exist.

The solar plexus is the great central sun or Dynamo, in which the subconscious mind, or we could call it the Divine Mind or the Mind of God, operates and causes the concept of individual consciousness.

Specifically stated thus:

1. The upper brain (cerebrum), the Most High or Universal Father, furnishes substances for all functions that constitute the body.

2. The Spiritual (I Exist) resident in the cerebellum

3. The Son of God, the redeeming seed, is born monthly in the solar plexus.

4. Soul, the fluids of the body.

5. Flesh, bone, etc., the fluids materialized. (In a broader sense, the body is also termed "soul," "Every soul," meaning every person.

No wonder the seer and alchemist of old declared that our bodies are the temple of the Living God, and the Kingdom of heaven is within us. But man, blinded by selfishness, searches here and there, looking through the heavens with his telescopes, digs deep into the earth, and dives into oceans depths in a vain search for the tonic of life that can be found between the soles of his feet and the crown of his head. Really, our human body is a miracle of mechanisms. No physical work of man can compare with the accuracy of its process and the simplicity of its laws.

At maturity, the human skeleton contains about 165 bones so delicately and perfectly adjusted that science has given up hope of ever imitating it. The muscles are about 500 in number. The length of the alimentary canal is 32 feet; an average adult's blood is 30 pounds or one-fifth of the body's weight. The heart is 6 inches long and four inches in diameter and beats 70 times per minute, 4200 times per hour and 100,800 times per day, and 36,720,00 times per year. At each beat, 2 1/2 ounces of blood are thrown out of it, 175 ounces per minute and 656 pounds per hour, or about 8 tons per day. All the blood in the body passes through the heart every three minutes, and it lifts 270,000,000 tons of blood for seventy years.

The lungs contain one gallon of air at their usual degree of inflation. We breathe, on average, 1200 breaths per hour; we inhale 600 gallons of air, or 24,000 gallons daily. The aggregate surface of the air cells of the lungs exceeds 20,000 square inches, an area nearly equal to that of a room twelve feet square.

Without going through the entire body, and its systems, we are definitely wonderfully made.
 There is not known in all the realms of architecture mechanics little device which is not found in the human organism. The pulley, the lever, the inclined plane, the hinge, the universal joint tubes and trap doors; the

scissors, grindstone whip, arch girders, filter, valves, bellows, pump, the camera, and Aeolian harp; irrigation plant telephone systems, telecommunication systems – all these and a hundred other devices which man thinks he invented, but which have only been telegraphed to the brain from the Solar Plexus (cosmic center) and crudely copied or manifested on the objective canvas (Spirit, slowed down to visibility).

No arch ever made by man is as perfect as the arch formed by the upper ends of the two legs and the pelvis to support the right of the trunk. Every palace or cathedral has been provided with a perfect system of arches and girders.

No waterway on earth is so complete, spacious, or populous as that wonderful river life, the "Stream of Blood." The violin, the trumpet, the harp, the grand organ, and all the other musical instruments are mere counterfeits of the human voice.

Another marvel of the human body is the self-regulation process by which our inner Source keeps the temperature in our health at 98 degrees. Whether in India, with the temperature at 130 degrees, or in the arctic regions, where the records show 120 degrees below freezing, the body's temperature remains the same, practically stead at 98 degrees, despite the extreme to which it is subjected.

In 1175, Alain deLille, a French theologian and poet, first recorded the proverb, "All Roads Lead to Rome." The early Alchemist and many Comforter Messengers discovered all roads of actual (spiritual) knowledge lead to the human body. The human body is an archetype of the universe. When Mankind turns with the powerful searching's of reason and investigation that they have so long used without – the "New Heaven and Earth" will appear visibly.

The nerves of our body constitute the "Tree of Life," with its healing leaves. The flowing waters of the "Rivers of Life" are the veins and arteries through which sweep the red, magnetic currents of Love; Spirit made visible.

Then we behold the Divine telecommunication system; the million never wires running throughout the wondrous temple we are, the temple not made with hands, the temple made "without the sound of saw or hammer."

Now view the Dynamo of Father; you may see the Beasts that worship before the Thorne day and night saying, "Holy, holy, is Though, Lord God Almighty." The Beasts are the twelve plexuses, nerve centers, and telecommunications stations, like the twelve zodiac signs that join hands in a fraternal circle across the gulf of space.

Aviation, liquified air, deep breathing for physical development, and the healing of diverse diseases rule the day. In every brain, dormant cells await Contact with the Divine Mind, releasing the vibration that will resurrect them. Everywhere we have evidence of the awakening of dormant brain cells. Science in every area is tapping into the Divine Mind / Father and practicing out of other than just physical knowledge (supernatural). We are seeing things we never dreamed of before; many, if not all, discoveries today are from the direct influence of spiritual awakenings brought into the use of once-dormant brain cells.

The Ancients and some modern-day Scientists, along with Comforter Messengers of our day, have discovered that there are dormant or undeveloped brain cells in countless numbers, especially in the cerebrum, or upper brain, the seat of moral faculties, or, more definitely speaking, the key, which, when touched with the vital force set free through the process of physical regenerating by the saving seed and by the baptism in ointment (Chrism) in the spinal cord, lifts the Chrism substance wasted by the prodigal son who did not know what he had, up to the Divine Brain. This release of the Chrism causes the dormant cells and little buds to actually bloom. The cells, while dormant, are like a flow yet in the bud. When the Chrism reaches them, the cells bloom and then vibrate at a rate that causes Consciousness of their eternal Newness of life. This is what Kay Fairchild calls "The Virgin Consciousness." It is no longer interpenetrated by carnally mindful knowledge and understanding.

We are in the age of Aquarius. During this Aquarian age, a significant correction in nature's laws will be speedily brought to pass, and substantial changes in the affairs of humanity will result. We see so much today that seems to be falling apart. In truth, what needs to be built and planted cannot be done until there is rooting out, pulling down, destroying, and throwing down that which hinders. This is what is taking place in people's awareness all over this planet. I believe the laws of Spirit, some say vibration, are being mastered by many. Through their operation, material manifestations of Spirit will be shaped and molded into being. We must see that all required from physical and spiritual life is already ours and always here, within us and without. Did not Jesus function out of his true supply? He often supplied more fish, bread, and other things, seemingly out of the air. It is well known by chemists that all manner of fruits, grains, and vegetables are produced directly from the elements in the air and not from the soil.

**There's an interesting verse of scripture in Luke 8:15, "But that on the good ground (higher thoughts) are they, which in an honest and good heart, having heard the (Living) word, keep it, and bring forth fruit with patience." KJV**

Good ground or higher thoughts come from meditation, but meditation takes patience. Jesus said, "If your eye be single, your whole body will be full of wisdom, knowledge, and understanding (light)," but it does take some patience. The war is patience. True meditation is vital to experience all Father wants for us. What we need to do, rather than just singing songs about "He is Lord, He is Lord," is to pay attention to what Jesus said, as recorded in Luke 6:46, "And why, call you me, Lord, Lord, and do not the things which I say?" KJV

What did Jesus tell us? He told us to meditate, he told us to turn within, he told us to go into the prayer closet (within) and shut out everything from the outside, and he told us to become little children.

"What are the characteristics of a little child? They trust mom and dad; even when turmoil is going on, they can be on the floor playing with toys and not paying attention. They don't worry. They're not anxious. They don't have anxiety attacks every day of their life. Why? Because they really draw, in a sense, from the right side (the Christ-Mind) more than they draw from the left side (lower thoughts)." #drkayfairchild From volume 2, Mind/Brain Connection - The Allegorical Reality of the Book of Revelation

Nov. 26th, 2021

This morning, in my dream state, I heard a female Messenger's calm and beautiful Voice say, "There is something between the Seer and the Eye." I take that to mean we are all spiritual Seers but we need our single-eye to be fully open. I'm guessing what was said to be between the Seers and the Eye," is all these non-powers many are focusing on.

PS- When scripture talks about vision, it's actually talking about the same vision Father has. How we see father, how we see ourselves, and how we see others.

## WAR AND PEACE

People desire world peace, but it will never come through the defeat or victory of any nation. Anyone who knows any history whatsoever will know that is true. We have always known war somewhere. World peace cannot be achieved by any nation's defeat or any nation's victory. We are a government of the Lord, and we need to know these things. Until the truth of both defeat and victory is relinquished, we will never know world peace. Nations, including the United States, have always argued about armament or disarmament. Some countries have thought if they are intensely armed with bombs and weapons, other governments would be afraid of them. Some nations have taken up the idea of disarmament thinking it will bring about world peace. Armament nor disarmament, defeat nor victory of any country will ever bring about world peace. History has proven that neither course provides the answer. There have been times when nations were heavily armed and then times when nations have been disarmed, but there was still war.

Another piece of history is back in 1914. England possessed the greatest navy and the greatest concentration of arms on the face of the globe. Even that did not prevent World War I. Then, later on, at the beginning of World War II, England was practically without arms, but this did not prevent war. We hear a lot today about gun control. Having a gun or not having a gun will not keep people from getting in trouble. It is not about that. Just the fact that people believe that either armament or disarmament will save them proves that they are headed for another war.

Why is there war rather than world peace? What is the origin of bad? The source of bad is the universal belief in two powers. We need to realize that we are the government of Father in earth, and we bring Peace to bear to this earth because we are called the Prince of the earth, and we should be the Prince of peace and perfection since we are the corporate Prince. We disagree with people who say we cannot have world peace. The Word says there will be a government—a shoulder people or an in Contact with the Divine Mind (Father) people—who will bring about the government of Father upon this earth. It will be through people who realize that the government we see out in the lower realm is absolutely a nonpower. Oh, it looks powerful and sounds powerful, but it is no power. We need to realize that the kingdoms of this world have become the kingdoms of our Father and His Sons and Daughters.

Jesus said if His servants were of this world, they would fight (see John 18:36). That is what people do; they fight because they are very much of this world. The fact is we are in the world, but not of it. There has to be a peaceful Solomon company coming on the scene who has their level of consciousness raised to the fact that Father is the only power and that constant Contact with Father/Divine Mind is their life. There is a nonpower in the world that would like us to believe that it has all power. We have to see the nonpower. People do not like this nonpower understanding because what they have feared looks real. Again, Jesus said that we are not of this world (see John 17:14), so He had to do something about it. He did what he revealed and taught. He said, "I have overcome the world" (John 16:33).

What if the only thing that's wrong with you, is because someone told you there is, so you think there is something wrong with you? Selah

**From my book of Revelation, translations:**

Revelation 5:11, "And I became aware of and heard in my thoughts, illuminating and thundering Voice's sounding as the Voice of One, being spoken through an innumerable number of people expressing Life, coming from every direction, and all around the Comforter Messengers, and those who responded to the Holy Breath in the Bride, saying, "Come and See". The numbers of those Voices were millions of times millions, times millions of millions; an immeasurable number of Father's creation, in contact and perfect fellowship with Father." They were singing, "Only Father receives the credit and admiration, for the reason being, His Great, and Marvelous Work from eternity (power) remains for ALL, eternally, age after age after age, world without end. What Father decided, decreed, and declared from eternity, is trustworthy, and worthy of putting one's entire being and life in the trust of. Bless His Holy Name." RERichmond Tree of Life Bible Translations

**I'm reminded that Jesus said, as recorded in John 10:11, "I exist one good shepherd: a good shepherd giveth his life for the sheep."**

Everything Jesus said of himself, like, I exist, the way, the truth, the life, and a good shepherd," was not saying he was the only one. He was telling the people he "existed" as those things, and so can we.

Jesus gave his life to those he taught, and so have others in history. However, "giving your life for those you teach" does not always mean your physical life. After "Fathers awareness," most pastors give up their life by giving up time with family, friends, and themselves.

Scripture states, "They are worthy of double honor."

1 Timothy 5:17 Let the elders/pastors who rule well be counted worthy of double honor, especially those who labor in the word and doctrine. 18 For the scripture saith, Thou shalt not muzzle the ox that treadeth out the corn. And The laborer is worthy of his reward. KJV

We know our Father is infinitely good. Once, they came to Jesus, called Jesus good, and he said, "There is none good but the Father." Jesus was not using the word "good," like the difference between good and bad. The term "good" is a higher realm of good. In the New Testament, there are two words for "good." One is agathos (ag-ath-os'), and it is the sense of a noun, as a person. The other is kalos (kal-os'), which means good in a moral sense or virtuous. Agathos is the God of sound, and kalos is simply from the appearance realm of good. Therefore, a Good Shepherd is as good as Father.

One of the meanings of "good" in Greek is "appealing." In other words, He is very appealing. The Message of the Gospel, ministered correctly, is appealing. It is not appealing when one instructs people to work to gain righteousness and favor from God. "Rules on rocks" are not appealing to anyone. However, explaining God as infinitely good, having nothing except love for His people, is very appealing to the hearer. When we teach the Truthful Gospel with great explanation, it will appeal to people.

Jesus willingly allowed the Pharisees and Sadducees to take him to the Romans to be put to death. He did this so that those he taught and others could have the opportunity to live an authentic life without depending on him as their daily provider. By doing this, they would be able to access their spiritual resources and not be dependent on what they thought they did not have. So, let us not squander this chance by simply asking for what we think we are lacking. We have all we need for physical and spiritual life, for it is all part of the same Life. Selah

For those of us who are of the Household of faith and acknowledge the Father's decision, decree, and declaration over mankind, we know that when we need an Angel/Messenger to come on the scene, they will be there. We need them in our daily lives, and David wrote this in Psalm 91:11 - "For God shall send Comforter Messengers: prophets, priests or teachers to establish you, to guard you with understanding, and wisdom in your entire life." RERichmond Tree of Life Bible Translations

These Messengers will raise your awareness and understanding, removing any sense of lack or defeat in your daily walk. It brings excellent guidance and protection when we embrace what they teach and explain.

We may not always be aware of the Messengers in our lives, but we have faith that Father is our protection and will always direct and guide us through Consecrated Comforter Messengers. Do you have one or more in your life, or even better, are you living as a Consecrated Comforter Messenger to help others?

I recently talked with a friend about why many people raised in Western Evangelical Christian Religions "unconsciously" prefer Jesus over Father.

I immediately heard, "It is because they put Jesus in the Mother's place, of an earthly Father and Mother relationship." I thought, "Wow, that's it!"

Almost all children prefer their Mother over their Father because their Mother is the one who cuddles them, comforts them when they hurt, cooks meals for them, and so forth. Father? He is the one "Who will spank you when he gets home when you've done something wrong." Father loves you but is portrayed as more of an authoritative figure in the family unit.

(Yes, I know Father and Mother relationships have changed a lot in our day, but I'm using this as a physical picture of spiritual truth.)

Our many versions of the Word of God project the same between our Eternal Father and Jesus. The many Bible translations show Jesus as a "Provider when you have a need; comforter when you are hurting; Counselor when you need advice, and rescuer when you are in trouble."

Father? The Bible translations reveal Father as "wrathful," "angry," often filled with "indignation," and if you do not follow His rules, you will suffer on earth, and after you die (all not true), but don't forget, Father loves you!

Jesus came to reveal the true character and nature of the Father by showing us Father in him and telling us we have Father in us. Jesus never wanted us to make statues of him, the cross's with him hanging on them, and hang a picture on our walls that we think looks like him. Jesus never portrayed Father as needing to be feared by anyone. Jesus always said what he heard Father say, which was nothing but love, and he always did what he saw Father do: love for ALL His children.

In John 8:31, Jesus did not say, "And you shall know the truth, and the truth shall make you free." He said, "And you are aware, have the knowledge, can speak of and understand the not-concealing Word and the not-concealing Word liberates and makes you exempt from ceremonial or mortal liability laws, and you can LIVE unrestrained."

If you follow a teacher, first because of their gender, you are missing the whole thing. In contact with Father, there is no gender; there is just one.

That blows away the old, worn-out belief that women can't teach or preach. And also, does away with ones "individual preferences." We must seek to hear the Voice of One, not gender or personality.

Physicist William Bray says, "You are not who or what you think you are. You are an eternal being, constructed of pure and unconditional love, constructed by God, and by human standards, you are all-knowing –right now….You are, in fact, standing in the Kingdom of God at this very moment, having a 'false perception' of being limited, separate from God, and even powerless. This is not the case. You are an infinite being who existed long before the Universe was created and will continue to exist, as yourself, for infinity, to the extent that this Universe is so infinitesimal in duration it does not even occur….If you are an artifact of the physical universe, then you are an artifact of a finite thing that does not truly exist (zero), and you, therefore, do not exist (an artifact of zero). You either exist for infinity, or you do not exist. You did not begin to exist at birth; neither can you cease to exist forever."

Did you happen to know? Water baptism symbolizes the cleansing of the awareness process by letting go of thought errors. It is the first step in the realization of Truth. My process started in 1988. It is pouring into consciousness the dissolving power of the Living Word, which breaks up and washes away all thoughts that are not the Truth. Water baptism in the Living Word is "putting on" the correct awareness; hence, the Living Word of Truth. Spiritual baptism is taking on an affirmation and letting go of the great lie of separateness. All growth occurs through these two attitudes – putting on and naturally letting go of all that hinders your thoughts. Religiosity tells us we need to let go first, then put on. The Apostle Paul always wrote, "Put on," and letting go will occur naturally. Hence, Jesus said, "The Truth (not-concealed Word), will make you free." So, we do not have to deal with the old thoughts, we just put on the Truthful thoughts, and the old will be defeated and melted away.

You have heard the following statement by Jesus so much that the real meaning might not be affecting you YET!

"You exist to know the Truth, and the Truth exists to make you free."

The Greek meaning of the word, the Greeks translated as "truth," is "the not-concealed Word." We know we are the Living Word, so when the wrong awareness concealment is removed, we will experience being the Living Word in our whole being.

I am reminded of what King Solomon told the Shulamite. He said, "Honey, you are a garden enclosed and a well shut-up." In other words, "Your awareness keeps you enclosed and shut up." Finally, she listened to him, believed what he declared over here, saw it, and danced over the hills (the heavenly awareness).

I have explained the word "name" as used in the phrase "Jesus' name" meaning "nature," as in prayer in Jesus' nature and way. The word 'name' to the ancients denoted "way." Therefore, the 'name of Jesus' infers doing things his way or as he did. It means to Seek first the kingdom of God (going deeper into one's self), and his righteousness and all things from within will be unfolded. It means: Entering the prayer closet (within) and closing the door to appearances. It means: Taking no thought of outer realm things which appear. Practicing seeing with your single eye causes the body to be filled with light. It means Meditation. It means: Saying only what we hear Father say and doing only what we see Father do.

That is the reality of the "Name of Jesus" rather than a phrase we begin or end our prayers with. We have certainly seen the results of speaking that name in prayer, but to truly experience the 'fruit that remains,' we follow his 'way' of life. Living the in-contact life, or our lives as Jesus did, makes all the difference in manifestation.

While reading the post of my FB connections, I found one by a person who commented about Romans 8:1-3, concerning many translators of the Bible, leaving out, "Who walk not after the flesh, but after the Spirit." He needed to explain why the long phrase was left out. The following are the answers:

The reason "they" left that phrase out is that the translators added all the words. You probably know this, but when looking at the bible words in Greek or Hebrew, if you find a word with the numerical number 9999, it means it was added by the translators.

I have attached a snippet of verse one for those who read this can see what words were added. When you remove the added words, you find, "No, therefore now, condemnation (self-imposed) to them in Christ Jesus. (Period) "In" comes from a Greek word, meaning "at rest," and "Christ" comes from the Greek root word Chrio, meaning "contact." So, if we are in contact with Father / Divine Mind, as Jesus was, then we would never self-condemn ourselves or allow anyone else to condemn us based upon their laws of religiosity.

Father never "condemned or condemns" anyone; only the "religions of this word" and their followers do (out of ignorance as to who and what Father really is).

I have translated all of the Letters of Paul to the Roman believers. The following is of Letter 3:1-5: 1 If you understood and embraced the last seven sections of my Letter which I wrote to you, and for future generations, age after age, you will know and believe the following. No person, not even one, ever needs to fear receiving an adverse sentence from our Father Creator, nor do they need ever to experience the resulting self-condemnation coming against them, which comes with fear. They all are just as Jesus was in His eternally fixed position of being ONE with our Father and Creator. There is no separation between the Father and humankind. There has never been, nor will there ever be.

Verse 2, NOW, the intensified prescription of living out of our Holy Breath for Life, just as Jesus lived, has delivered us all from the prescription of the Mosaic Law. We are free from the drudgery of offering dead animals, bloody sacrifices, seeds, fruits, gold, and silver to Father for appeasement. 3 The Law of Moses was a sensual, impotent, impossible prescription. It could never accomplish its goal since it had no life. It was sickly and without strength because of the ineffectual, dead animals and bloody sacrifices. But on the contrary, One Father, embodied as Jesus, in and through Jesus' incarnational events, did what the law could never do. First, He revealed His eternal love for all humanity. Then He condemned and repealed the Mosaic prescription of the continual offering of animal sacrifices, which people did to appease Father. Father, in Jesus, drew all the consequences of mistaken identity and took the many prescriptions of dead works into himself. In His act of dying, all the false awareness in man died. 4 He did all that, so the determination, decision, and decree Father gave from the foundation could finally be experienced by all people. His prescription showed us how to live out of our HOLY BREAT for (Zoe) Life. His intention was not for us to follow the Mosaic remedies to gain wholeness of Life, but He planned for all people to live out of Holy Breath / Father, who is our life, to experience fullness, since IT provides everything required for physical and Spiritual Life. 5 People who continue after the prescription of dead animals and bloody sacrifices are mindful of the "do to be" laws. They are unsuccessfully trying to produce what they already possess. They are already righteous. They are already one with Father. They think they are appeasing an angry Father. They believe He wants people to offer these sacrifices to Him, but He doesn't. But those who live from the Spirit Life resource have an awareness full of Truth. They are living out of their spiritual resources for Life. RERichmond Tree of Life Bible Translations.

| | Οὐδὲν | ἄρα | νῦν | κατάκριμα | τοῖς | | ἐν | Χριστῷ | Ἰησοῦ. | | | | | | | | |
|---|---|---|---|---|---|---|---|---|---|---|---|---|---|---|---|---|---|
| There is | no | therefore | now | condemnation | to them | which are | in | Christ | Jesus, | who walk | not | after | the | flesh, | but | after | the | Spirit. |
| 9999 | 3762 | 686 | 3568 | 2631 | 3588 | 9999 | 1722 | 5547 | 2424 | <9999> | <9999> | <9999> | <9999> | <9999> | <9999> | <9999> | <9999> | <9999> |
| | Oudén | ára | nūn | katákrima | toís | | en | Christoó | Ieesoú | | | | | | | | |

Have you wondered what the Greek word meant, that "they" translated as "forgive"?

In every instance where the KJV uses the word "forgive," referencing Jesus' statements, the Greek word is aphiemi, meaning to "send forth" what is hindering you. The following is an example of what is commonly called "The Lord's Prayer." (Jesus' prayer was in John 17)

When Jesus taught how to converse with Father, he said, as recorded in Matthew 6:9-12 "Father, we are one in perfect rest, as you are Spirit, we are Spirit; holy and pure is our nature. Your nature is apparent in and as us. Our righteousness was caused to be from the foundation by your determination, decree, and purpose by you; in that same manner from the foundation, it is eternally true, of everyone. That which is required daily is supplied. Our substances are bestowed day after day. Also, you SEND FORTH (forgive) our belief of needing to appease you, and in the same manner, we SEND FORTH that sense of needing of others to appease us. RERichmond Tree of Life Bible Translations

Once we understand what Jesus really said, we should never need to "forgive" anyone because, out of our true nature and character, we hold nothing against anyone.

It is vital that "we all" allow our Holy Breath to vitalize our individual awareness.

Those who have the eternal love of the Father vitalized in their awareness (heart) are not disturbed by the lower thoughts; they have passed over to the Truth of the Living Word and leave out the lower thoughts that always traduce. When all the desire of our Divine Mind is allowed to be in the complete dominion of one's individual awareness, to only express Father, then the person will experience their eternal wholeness and seeing with their seeing – single-eye.

As recorded in Matthew chapter 13, Jesus was asked by his disciples why he spoke to the people in parables. Jesus answered their question from verses 11 to 15, and then he told them in verse 16, ""Supremely blessed, happy, fortunate, well off is the eye, that looks and perceives and the ear, to hear" (Matt. 13:16 RERichmond Tree of Life Bible Translations).

I discovered, in Hebrew, the word "enmity" is hatred for another race or tribe. So, when one practices racism they make Father in another form, color, creed, race, country, or nation rather than One people. If you are a racist or a religionist, you are at enmity against Father's nature and image in mankind.

**True Circumcision – what is it?**

To the Religious Leaders of the Jews, and to those who try to follow the law of Moses and the law minded-man:
Romans 2:17 You proclaim yourselves to be leaders and rest in the law of Moses by boasting that your law is the way to know and please Father. 18 You believe you know Father's will, according to your documents concocted by man, and you believe it to be excellent in bringing instruction and correction to others. 19 You act confident that you are a guide for those you think have no ability to see that which is spiritual and try to teach a shining revelation for those who supposedly do not have any revelation knowledge. 20 You promote yourselves as higher than others in awareness. You treat those you

instruct as mindless. You, fashion and present yourself to have the knowledge and know the truth in the law. However, you have no true knowledge whatsoever; you think your law is the final word.

Verse 21, Accordingly, with what you think you know, you teach others. You should teach those things you preach to yourself. You teach others not to steal. Do you steal? 22 You teach others not to commit sexual sins. However, by obeying your law, you cannot control your sensual desires. You are disgusted with the idolatry of others, but you are a temple robber of the pagans. 23 You, who are caught up in the Law of that which was put together by Moses, and the additional laws added by other men, boast of how you follow every part of the law and declare that it is of Father. Through violation of your law, in not doing it, you dishonor yourself and the true and living Father. Father is not the author of your law, nor the author of Moses' law.

Verse 24, For the true nature and character of Father is blasphemed through your speaking impiously against those who are not Jews, as you inscribe the way of life your law promotes. 25 Circumcision is advantageous to satisfy your teachers if you keep Moses' law, but if you break any of Moses' laws or any of those laws you added, then it is as though you were not circumcised – it is useless. 26

Conversely, if those who do not practice circumcision live the righteous life the law tries to produce, shall their uncircumcision not be counted for circumcision? Father never required circumcision of any part of the body. Do you think obeying every part of the law makes you righteous?

27 Those people who are not circumcised, who are living out of their true nature, who are not doing things which break your law, shall they make a decree and decide against you Jews, who attempt to follow the law of Moses' and other men? Shall they charge you, who are circumcised, who continue to violate and constantly fail at obeying these laws? 28 Therefore, I boldly declare to you all, who are following the "do to be" rules of righteousness, which are an outward effort: it does not make you spiritual Israel, and it does not make you one who lives and rules as Father; neither does circumcision, which is another "do to be" effort. 29 But he who truly lives as spiritual Israel, one who lives and rules as Father, is one inwardly, ruling his earthen vessel and the world, as Father

Verse 29, Those who truly live as Spiritual Israel do so from an inward source. They possess power as princes of this earth and rule as Father with strength and ability, which comes from the Source within. Legalistic circumcision sought but failed to produce righteousness. The true sense of righteousness can only come from the thoughts and feelings in one's conscious awareness that flows from their Holy Breath. Righteousness cannot come from the letter of the Law and circumcision. No credit whatsoever is to be given to men who draw from physical, sensory information and promote "do to be" laws. One hundred percent of the credit is given to our Father. Father never required circumcision; it came from Abraham's upbringing, through his Ur of Chaldean background; it was his idea that he accredited to Father, not Fathers. RERichmond Tree of Life Bible Translations

I was meditating on what I was going to teach, and this thought came to me: "Look up Psalm 122:1 and translate "let us go unto..."

I discovered a hidden nugget. The Hebrew phrase, "Let us go unto," is "Let us walk." So, we can say, "I was glad (relieved) when they told me, let us walk as the house of Father."

Don't throw your bibles away; there are thousands of hidden golden (Divine) nuggets to mine out in each book.

Did you happen to know? What Father says today is what Father said from the foundation. Father speaks to your thoughts, and what you hear sounds like your voice, but if you are attuned to your Divine Mind, you know it is Father speaking. Father speaks through Sons and Daughters, Comforter Messengers, who are people, and through all creation.

Father's voice is like a sound or word we make - it never ceases; it keeps going through space as a vibration. So, what Father decided, declared, and decreed from the foundation is still speaking and only heard when one tunes to the correct frequency. To me, the frequency is Father's eternal love. Father always speaks, from eternity - can you hear?

Father never "promised" mankind anything. Father declared all we have and are to be so. Father's declarations are eternal and continue in all people, "world without end."

If we wait for Father "to do something" or "give something," we miss out on what Father declared from eternity. "We HAVE all things that pertain to physical and spiritual life." What we have, is not based upon what we see with our physical eyes.

**Relieved by the Truth**

**Jesus told his disciples; he would not leave them "comfortless." Many teachers teach the word "comforter" as being "the Holy Spirit."**

Jesus said, "But this one, and many other relievers, being himself Holy Breath, sent by Father in the same spiritual authority I possess; "He" and "they" shall teach and explain the whole of what I sought to teach and explain to you. He will bring to remembrance all whatsoever I said unto you. John 14:26 RERichmond Tree of Life Bible Translations.

The Greek word translated as "comforter" is parakletos, which is an intercessor or consoler (reliever - ray of sunshine). The Apostle Paul and many others defiantly are a ray of sunshine, to those who were, and still are, in the darkness of religiosity.

I lived over half my life believing the comforter was our Holy Breath, and "I had to receive the Holy Spirit" and then speak with an "unknown language" to prove I possessed Father's Holy Breath. I discovered that my entire life, I contained Holy Breath! In fact, I was eternally in Father (Holy Breath/Spirit).

A Comforter is a person with spiritual understanding and brings the realization of man's inherent Father/Source/Papa character and nature. The Comforter is a Messenger/Teacher, attuned to the inner presences of Holy Breath, Chi, Essence, Divine Sources, and Divine Mind (all are one and the same).

When we have taken the external steps toward a renewed individual awareness, divinely aligning our consciousness, we begin to know we are not left alone in our effort to behold and express ourselves spiritually. We become aware we are being companioned by Holy Breath in our Thoughts and Comforter Messengers, who guard and guide us as the light of love, being taught in the Truthful Living Words. We are "comforted" by what we become aware of, and the Truth will make us experience who we really are and divinely correct our perception of the Father.

This teaching, this light, this love comes from within. Jesus called them the intercessor, consoler (reliever - ray of sunshine), teachers, and explainers who are Holy Breath as you are Holy Breath because what they teach and what you hear from the Voice of Father, soothing, strengthening, quiet, and calm, which reveals something we can depend on.

Therefore, we are all Holy Breath; many of us are mandated to be Comforter Messengers of the Living Word. I am thankful for my many Comforter (relievers) Messengers. I was relieved for the first time when I heard the Truthful Living Word.

I was relieved when I heard I Exist as the house of the Lord.
I was relieved when I heard I Exist eternally righteous and Holy.
I was relieved when I heard Father was never angry with me, nor could be.
I was relieved when I discovered the words "wrath" and "indignation" were wrongly translated from a word that meant
 "Longing for Love of Father."

I was relieved when I discovered Father eternally provided (saved) for me, from eternity, that I lack nothing. I was relieved when I found the "foreign language" that people need to hear is the language of Fathers' eternal love for all persons; a world without end.

I was relieved when I heard, "Let us boldly enter into the awareness that we are Father's dwelling place, and we live as the Face of Father."

I could pen thousands of truths I have discovered that brought and continues to bring great relief to my awareness.

Are you relieved by what you are taught, hear, believe, and see? If not, join us as we enter the great cloud of Witnesses in their awareness.

**Abaddon, a-bad'-don, means destroyer; destruction. In Greek, Abaddon was said to be king over a great army of locusts that came out from the abyss to destroy (Rev. 9:2-11).**

The Spiritual symbolism of Abaddon is this name has reference to a very destructive belief of man whose understanding comes from sensory knowledge and is evident from the meaning of the name and from the 9th chapter of Revelation.

From Exodus 10:14, 15 and Joel 2:3-10, in comparing these texts with their references above, you will see that they all are speaking of the same thing. One can get an idea of the destructiveness of the locusts of Palestine and the surrounding countries. They commonly came up like great armies and ate every living plant in their path; also, including the leaves and the branches of the trees.

Branches, leaves, and trees all symbolize those supposed to be teachers of righteousness.

So, Abaddon must stand for the error of belief in the utter destruction of life and form.

The true-life principle can never be destroyed; only the outer form of man's belief in materiality is destructible. So long as man believes in materiality or destruction, the outer destruction of forms will take place. It is vital, therefore, that the thought of the possibility of life's being destructible or in any way limited be erased entirely from the consciousness. There is only one Presence, Mind, and Power in the universe, and IT is Father in and as us.

Life is omnipresent, eternal, and sure; life cannot be destroyed because it is God Himself.

"The difference between Western Evangelical Christianity and the Eastern approach to Truth is like the difference between talking about a meal and eating a meal."

I prefer to "Taste and see that our Father is nothing but good."

**Humility**
In Genesis 49:27, Jacob is talking to his son Benjamin. Benjamins' name means "Son of the right hand; dexterous, skillful, expert, and quick." Jacob gives Benjamin a prophecy fulfilled in Paul, a Benjamite. He told Benjamin he would be like a wolf providing food for its pups. Food is a symbol of appropriation of the Living Word. In the morning (time of great light – understanding), he would

eat (study) the prey, and at night (places where people had no light – understanding), he would provide (teach) the food to all who were hungry. When the Apostle Paul was apprehended by what Jesus taught him, he devoured it for over three years. Later, he fed portions to those who had none initially.

Then in Genesis 44:2, we find a cup in Benjamin's sack. We know that cup was a silver cup, which was empty. Silver is the biblical metal that represents redemption. In Hebrew, the word "redemption" infers a relationship (OT:1353 geullah (gheh-ool-law' - relationship). In Greek, "redemption" means riddance (NT:629 apolutrosis (ap-ol-oo'-tro-sis -riddance), as in removing something that hinders. Redemption has nothing to do with an act of salvation, like being saved from punishment.

The Apostle Paul fulfilled this prophecy. Father placed in Paul a Benjamite message, which is a perfect understanding of what Jesus revealed to the people. He sought to show everyone's perfect Oneness with Father (relationship). Jesus' passion removed (riddance) from the people that traduced or hindered them, which was their perceived mistaken identity. Religiosity taught a false identity and perception of who Father was, along with many other great lies.

The cup in Benjamin's sack represented Jesus's consciousness of eternal Life. This consciousness is attained by coming out of personal self or ego – me, myself, and I. Jesus said, as recorded in John 18:11, "This is the cup which the Father has given me," meaning he did not have any personal ambition. Jesus' sole motive was to be FOR the people. Everything he did or said was to bless others. He never used his supernatural nature for his own benefit. I desire to do the same: have no personal ambition, bless others, and function supernaturally for the sake of other people.

The revelation was revealed to the Apostle Paul the Benjamite, and he clearly explained what was revealed to him. The translators, controlled by religiosity, distorted what he wrote.

Jesus took away (destroyed) all our confusion about our Father, our mistaken identity, and the resulting symptoms (behaviors). He dropped a silver relationship and riddance cup in the mouth of our sack. The symbology of the cup was to reveal spiritual truth to all who would pay attention. To drink of the cup from which Jesus drank is to 1) rise above all sense desires; 2) gain mastery over every impulse of that which is without; 3) devote one's whole life to that which is within, our Holy Breath and Divine Mind. The sack would be the Living Word of Truth in us that we are. The thing that opens the Word is the cup of relationship and riddance. Once we understand our Oneness with Father, the riddance of all that hinders is automatic. Thus, the cup is empty of everything but the relationship with our Abba.

I Desire To Do The Same: Have No Personal Ambition, Bless Others, And Function Supernaturally For The Sake Of Other People.

I am thankful that our Divine understanding is taking pieces of the puzzle of the Word and putting them in the proper perspective and priority they need to be placed. We thank our Father. We can see clearly now. The old perceptions are leaving, and we see that all obstacles in our way are gone. The dark rain-less clouds that held us blind are gone. It's become a bright, bright day we live in.

Clouds symbolize people; they either have rain (teaching) to pour out, or they are just rain-less clouds that are nice to look at but bring no nourishment (water of the Logos).

This continues to be true. Rain represents the living Logos taught as the creative spiritual law-giving and revealing activity in us all.

In every change of individual awareness on the physical plane, there is a breaking down of cells in our brain and a building up of other cells to take their place. Mentally this is denial and affirmation, and this process in the body results from these two movements in awareness. We let go of the mortal or human-minded life and take hold of the spiritual life by giving up consciously to this "passing over" process, which takes place when the old cells are replaced by the new.

During Israel's Passover, the lamb was killed and eaten in the night represents this giving up of the human-minded life in the obscurity of the carnal thought life. The command is that the lamb (us – Lambkin) shall be without spot or blemish and be "wholly, eaten after being roasted with fire, which is the Living Word. This refers to the complete surrender of the human-minded life after it has been purified by the Living Word of regeneration. Fire represents the Living Word affirmative state of mind, as opposed to the state of mind produced by embracing the written Word, with all its false perceptions and wrong translations.

Are you aware - All spiritual seekers of Truth have found by experience that being thankful for what they have increases the inflow? Gratitude is a great awareness magnet, and when it is expressed from a spiritual standpoint, it is powerfully augmented. Being grateful for what you have originates in this idea of the power of increase through giving thanks.

**When dining on much truth, love to share what I eat.**
Spiritual perception reveals that we are not just an "individual" person but factors in our Oneness with Father and each other. The real treasure is our Oneness. A revelation of "Oneness" with Father rids us of all that hinders us. Reveal your glory to yourself by affirming, "I am One with Father, a son or daughter of the living Source – Father of all things."

Look at yourself not as flesh and blood but as Holy Breath. Jesus affirmed his true self, and the Father acknowledged him. The reason for the limited comprehension and power of the dust-dweller man is that he sees the world about him as being under material law, and agreeing with it makes him part of it.

**From the parable of the "Good Samaritan."**

The road to Jericho from Jerusalem was a steep, treacherous path and even more dangerous because robbers were lying in wait for travelers. This condition was the setting where Jesus told several parables, including the one about the Good Samaritan.

The phrase, "On the road from Jericho," represents the external consciousness or realm of exhibited thought, and up to Jerusalem is our spiritual consciousness. Yes, these are dangerous places through which we must pass. The thieves and robbers we meet are thoughts of error that would turn us aside from the Living Word of Truth and dissipate the life substance of our actual being. "The thief (Mosaic Law & its loathsome fruit) cometh not, but that it may steal, and kill, and destroy, I came that they may experience and handle life (Zoe) and may handle and experience it abundantly" (John 10:10).

The greatest robber the race must deal with is the lie of religiosity and its many "do to be" laws. These 'do to be" prescriptions for life turn millions aside from seeking after the true life through the one Source (giver of life), which is our Father within us as our Holy Breath. The robber presents many erroneous religious ideas, which exalts death as the way to heaven and spiritual realization. These lead people to the grave and away from eternal life, knowing what Jesus taught and staying in constant contact with Father through our Divine Mind. We can find eternal life only by daily learning of the Truthful Word and dwelling in Contact with Father here and now, and not by letting go of the consciousness of Zoe Life. The pure, unadulterated Contact with our Divine Mind (Father) alone leads to the experience of Zoe Life within us. Thus, the reason Jesus said, "The unconcealed (not-Concealed) Word (truth) will cause us to experience (make) our eternal freedom, which will reveal to us the truth of who we are – Sons and Daughter of our Father – Papa."

This steep path on the road to Jericho symbolizes the place in our individual consciousness where erroneous thoughts are most likely to enter. It is called the Adummim. If we properly deal with the wrong ideas, we raise our awareness and ascend to the place or state of going up into LIFE. Those who do not deal with false beliefs fall into the hands of robbers. The robbers are teachers of the tree of the knowledge of good and bad. Those teachers infest the way, and it becomes a red place, which is the meaning of Adummim - red spots, place of the red ones, place of blood, red places.

Interestingly, the root word for Adummim is Adam', the name of the first race of man. It is also a place in Palestine, which means "dust dwellers." Palestine is only mentioned once in the Old Outlook and perception books and in the book of Joel. Biblical history states Palestine was in Syria, not Israel.

If we only study the Scripture on a surface level, as literal and moral, then, like many believers, we miss the spiritual truths of the matter and end up self-condemning ourselves and, worse, others. Approaching the Scripture intellectually, apart from Holy Breath, genders little wisdom and little proper understanding of the Living Word. This includes hearing Father, spiritually unintelligent.

**Something to think about:** When we approach a new experience from our Divine Mind Consciousness, we are hungry for the Truths it holds. For example, in our quest for Truth, we will undoubtedly believe our intentions are good. We usually start with a minimal foundation of Truthful principles but fail to deepen our spiritual understanding by exercising our constant contact with Father – our Divine Mind. We settle for religious bias instead of striving for a spiritual vision.

Many become quite satisfied with only a literal interpretation of Scripture and see no need to explore hidden Truths or fail to apply spiritual Truths. When these conditions exist, they represent a barren state of mind devoid of producing higher spiritual insights (a fruitless fig tree).

In Philippians 3:8, Paul said he counted everything he learned from the Law to be dung. He was speaking of his religiously interpenetrated thoughts and beliefs. The Apostle was preparing to cast all the dung entirely from his consciousness. He released the old mindset from his thoughts when realizing they were no longer of value to him.

Selah!

In conversations with people in person and worldwide via video or audio Messenger, I find most people believe Jesus' parables to be true stories. So much so they often place great fear and condemnation on people that they use the parables to cause them to "convert" to their belief systems.

**Have you wondered why Jesus spoke so many parables?**

Jesus desired to bring the truth to the people. That truth would make them free from the many bondages holding them back. Their inability for spiritual truths was the reason for many parables. The word "parable" comes from a compound Greek word parabola, meaning "to throw alongside." In other words, a parable is a story thrown alongside a more philosophical idea to illustrate it in familiar terms.

Parables are earthly stories illustrating heavenly truths, as in a fable. For example, has a better illustration ever been given of what it means to love one's neighbor than the story of the Good Samaritan? Or the example of the eternal love of the Father than the story of the Prodigal Son? Both were fables given to reveal spiritual truth. So, the parables (fable stories) exist to inform, clarify, and illustrate spiritual facts.

Our journey to raise our awareness is often better for us to examine a story that gives us a physical picture of the spiritual truth. Jesus gave them these stories and correlations because they stimulate higher consciousness. They trigger the hearer to want to learn more. Once our awareness rises to a higher level of spiritual truth, we begin to understand the hints of the Living Word of Truth, and our lives are greatly affected. However, focusing on the physical story of the parable instead of hearing the more remarkable Spiritual Truth of the Living Word hinders a person from hearing and listening to the Divine Wisdom, the real intent of the teaching.

The hearer often majors on the physical story more than the truth to which the parable points. We know this to be accurate because the majority who teach the parables of Jesus make them true accounts, as in the parable of the rich man and poor man, the woman at the well, the supposed "prostitute" taken to Jesus for judgment, and so forth. Most people believe the story or myth is genuine and do not glean the Spiritual Truth from it.

We would do well, always do better, if we look below the surface of the Living Word and discover the creative spiritual law giving and revealing activity in us, as the Book of Life we are.

**Are you worried about your life?**

Do not be worried about what you have or do not have that you can see but be about others' blessing."

The explanation: We don't always see what we have because there is no requirement for it at that moment. We are Cherubim, who are people of blessing. We are givers, not takers. That's why Jesus said giving out of our eternal abundance is much more enjoyable than receiving.

The veil of religiosity is rent in many lives today. It is rent by letting go of beliefs in the reality of material consciousness and awakening to the light of Holy Breath – Spiritual living. The final relinquishment of the soul of its self-identity is the absolute giving up of all self-serving human ambitions and aims. When a person reaches this point, their soul enters awareness of its glory.

**Did you know "present truth" is not what Father is "saying today?"**

Present truth is the eternal Living Word of Truth within every person.

How do we know if this to be true? Because "We have contact with our Father (Divine Mind) and we know all the Logos." 1 John 2:14 RERichmond Tree of Life Bible Translations

The answer to your question is that we need to be fully aware of all we know, but we will.

2 Peter 1:12, "Wherefore, I will not be negligent to put you always in remembrance of these spiritual teachings, though ye know them, and be established in the present truth."

The English word "present" comes from the Greek pareimi (par'-I'mee), meaning to be near, at hand, and also, I Exist. The word "truth" is the same word Jesus used when he said, "The truth will make you free," coming from the Greek alethes (al-ay-thace), meaning "true" as the not concealing Word. Peter was telling his students that the Living Word of Truth existed in them and was near at hand, meaning they could execute the Truthful Word in all their dealings and life.

Are you aware the Apostle Paul did not say, "To be carnally mindful is death," as in we have a carnal mind? Our mind is the Divine Mind because there is only one Mind.

Paul said, "To possess an inclination toward fleshly and lower understanding and things is to live AS you are dead to spiritual understanding. However, to possess an inclination toward spiritual understanding is to Live fully alive." [Translated and Paraphrased by me]

Have you heard the saying, "You are what you eat?" I would say, "Your realization is formed from what you eat."

We have, and many still live, in a day of the great famine of hearing the Truthful, Living Word. The famine is not because no one is teaching the Truthful, Living Word; it is because those stuck in the many doctrines of carnally mindful people refuse to listen.

Father inspired Hosea to write, "My people are dumb and silent to the truthful, Living Word because they failed to ascertain, seek and desire to know MY knowledge: because you have disdained truthful knowledge, your rejection has hindered you from the experience of being who I created you to be as Me. You have forgotten who you are and that I Exist in you and your children also." [Hosea 4:6 RERichmond Tree of Life Bible Translations and Paraphrased]

While studying, I was reminded of the appeal in scripture, "We have an unction of the Holy One, and we know all things." I've quoted that verse often.

Today I was impressed to look up the word "unction" in Greek and was surprised to discover it carries the same meaning as the word "christ - chrio: Both mean CONTACT.

The word "things" comes from a word that means "the whole," implying Logos. So, we can read the verse as "You have contact with Father (Divine Mind), and you know all the Living Word."

So, as I stayed quiet, I heard Father speak in my thoughts, "You know all my Living Word, but you are not fully aware right now, but I will continue to open up to you the awareness."

**This is a Truth:** John the Baptist, with his perception of the Truth, prepared the way for Holy Breath through the riddance of old concepts and beliefs. We are fully aware that Father is Holy Breath, and Breath is located and appears wherever IT is recognized by a wise person. IT thus follows whoever gives his or her attention to Holy Breath and seals his or her eternal identification with IT by Fathers eternal Living Word. IT starts a release and flow of Holy Breath life, and all the attributes of Holy Breath in and through his or her individual awareness becomes a moment-by-moment experience.

To the extent that mankind practices identifying with the One and only Divine Mind (Father - Source) of all existence, he or she experiences being Holy Breath, until finally, the awareness of Oneness with Father becomes their reality, in which he or she can say with Jesus, "I and the Father are one," and they are not just quoting Jesus; this truth has now become personalized.

**The Spiritual Symbology of the parable of the Merchant "seeking" a pretty (goodly) pearl and finding a pearl of great price.**

Matthew 13:45-46 Again, the kingdom of heaven is like unto a merchant man, seeking goodly pearls: Who, when he had found one pearl of great price, went and sold all that he had, and bought it. KJV

Knowing what the Kingdom of Heaven or of God is, we could say of this parable and the others, The rule and domain of the Divine Mind within us is like unto a...

Matthew 6:33 "But seek ye first the rule and domain of the Divine Mind within, and your equitable characters (righteousness); and all these things you think you need, shall be unfolded from out of the midst of you." RERichmond Tree of Life Bible Translations

To learn more, find my Face Book video teaching on this subject, May 29th, 2021.

Matthew 5:14 We are the light of the world. And when we express our true Divine Nature, everyone will see IT. 15 When we live, move, and have our being from that high spiritual consciousness, we cannot hide the intensity of our oneness with our Divine Mind (Father) because we are Holy Breath, and we are the Children of Light. We are Light, which is spiritual energy made visible. 16 We must let our Holy Breath within us reveal our oneness with Father. That which we know and believe must be the Driving Force of all we do so that others may also see their true Nature and turn to the same Light (Holy Breath) within them. Contrary to what many believe and teach, we are not "Spirits having a human experience." We are Holy Breath, experiencing the cool of the day. We are living and walking as the presence of our Father in every part of our being. We are Sons and Daughters of our Father/Creator and are in His perfect likeness. RERichmond Tree of Life Bible Translations

## Attention Pastors!

I was reminded of what Father instructed Jeremiah to say about giving Pastors after Fathers own individual awareness (heart). Jeremiah wrote, "I will give you pastors according to mine heart, which shall feed you with knowledge and understanding." The phrase, "according to mine heart," in this verse are feelings, will, intellect, and awareness."

As Pastors and Teachers, we must be aware of the Father's individual awareness of all people. Is what you teach and explain of Father honestly after Father's personal awareness, or is it of your individual awareness that has been affected by various religious beliefs?

Think about it; how do your followers feel after you teach or preach to them? Are the knowledge and wisdom you teach coming from Father's awareness (Living Word), or from only the written word?" Selah

I have sat under many teachers, who were not teaching me, according to Father's feelings, will, intellect, and awareness: I always left feeling ashamed and fearful.

Here is the problem. When a person spends a lifetime under teachings not representative of the Father's feelings toward them, will, intellect, and individual awareness of them, they become conditioned to the great lie and reject the truth when hearing it.

Let's ensure what we teach and preach is after Father's awareness. If it is, the Hearer will experience peace, perfection, and joy - no longer shame, doubt, and fear.

Have you heard a preacher talk about the word "Ichabod" as in meaning the glory of the Lord might leave you? I have, and as a young man, it always scared me that it could happen to me.

In Hebrew, you will find Glory means "Vision."

So rather than the Prophet of old saying Ichabod, the glory of the Lord has left this house, he said, "The vision of the Lord has left these people."

There again, the Bible is all about our awareness or vision. Interesting? Yes, it is!

**A new FB connection/brother told me, in the recent past, he had several dreams; he gave birth to a man-child; he wondered what it meant.**

The "man-child" is found in Revelation, when the Sun (Son-minded) clothed woman with a crown of twelve stars gives birth to a man-child. Religiosity try's to swallow it up when it is birthed, but it does not succeed.
The symbolism of a crown is either spiritual awareness or carnal awareness. This woman (no gender implied) possesses a spiritual awareness; hence, she is clothed in spiritual understanding.

Jesus bearing a crown of thorns symbolizes a carnal awareness; he bore that to free all people from the lie of being void of Father's life.

The person who gives birth to a man-child possess' s the twelve functioning, Divine facilities* and stays in constant contact with their Divine Mind (Father).

Giving birth is rising to the highest spiritual awareness. Being a man-child is the result of never leaving your birth state, being fully aware of Father and who you are; in all your ways, you are spiritually mature.

We all need to experience being "the man-child, living fully as a Daughter or a Son of a Father. Allowing the Voice of Father in the many Comforter Messengers to cloth and crown you will do excellent work. Your crown (understanding or awareness) will shine bright.

If your current crown still has thorns in it, it is high time you place the old crown (carnal awareness) at the feet of a Comforter Messenger and allows him or her to give you a bright and shiny crown with many jewels/stars (understandings).

**What is the "Law of Love?"**

Romans 13:1 Every person who masters their supernatural power automatically excels in being as Father. For there is no power but for Father, and Father is Holy Breath as we are, and ordained from the foundation to be the plural of Father. 2 So too, one who resist their Holy Breath and the Voice of Father, speaking to their thoughts or others, resist what our Father decided, decreed and declared from the foundation; "Father made man as the plural of Him." When one fights who they really are, they stand against themselves, to self-condemnation.

3 For Comforter Messenger, Teachers do not exist as ones who put people in fear to cause them to do good works. Therefore, they will not cause harm. Will you delight in your Holy Breath? Do not be afraid of your supernatural Self; you are beautiful and beneficial to others, and if you delight in who you are, you will be doing an admirable thing for others, not only yourself.

4 Father indeed attended to you, from the foundation to purpose well in your life forever. However, for any reason, one who resists you as Holy Breath will be goodly alarmed for him because it will not be in vain. The word you carry for the one who resists has the decision, decree, and declaration of Father from the foundation, that he or she too is the plural of Father, which is the message of love, not pouring out any harm on them.

5 Consequently, it is necessary to listen to the Voice of your Holy Breath with intelligence and be able to quickly repeat what was said not only in love for Father but for the sake of being aware of Father's purpose and speaking what you heard correctly.

6 Now, if you are served by a public minister, functioning as a teacher to you, pay him or her well, for they are consecrated of Father. They tirelessly attend all the exercises of attending to the welfare of the people by teaching and exhortations. 7 Pay them all they are due, honor and reference them, where money will not concern them.

8 Do not be indebted to one another but love one another: for he, that loveth another hath fulfilled the law of love. 8 Because of the law of love, this I tell you, you will not commit adultery, you will not kill one another, you will not steal anything, you will not covet what others have, because the real commandment is love, and in love, you discover none of those actions are of your nature and character; there will be no desire toward others, except for perfect love (agape). In loving others, you love yourself. 10 You, bestowing perfect love toward everyone, produce no worthless acts; in so doing, you fulfill the law of Love.

**I like this: Romans 8:35 -37**

Romans 8:35 What person or deed could ever have the ability to separate or put asunder this great and marvelous love, which our Wonderful, Great and Marvelous Father has for us all. Jesus revealed this love that Father had for all humanity? Can pressure from the world systems separate anyone from this wondrous love? No! Distress? No! Maltreatment from those who resist the Truth. No! Irrational fear? No! A strong sense of lack? No! Erroneously believing yourself to be a mere human? No! Life-threatening danger? No! The expectation of a religiously imposed punishment? No!

36 My mandate, mission, and ministry are engraved in my whole being for your sake. My fellow ministers and I offer our lives to you daily. Because of our mandate, we are accounted as non-resisting fodder for the butchery of those mindful of the Mosaic Law.

37 Nevertheless, in all this distress, maltreatment, and life threats, these things and more from those who do them are subdued and powerless because of our victory over them, revealed by Jesus' living mandate, mission, and ministry. Father is the one who eternally loved us. Jesus was victorious in what he was mandated to do; likewise, we are victorious we are mandated to do.

## The Mystery of Christ

One more mystery we were hidden from by the initiation of religious rites is the meaning of the word "Christ," which has brought great confusion to all who follow Jesus' teachings. I will not share much on this "once mystery" because I have shared the explanation many times over the past year.

A short explanation is many times, the word "Christ" was wrongly placed in many sentences, and the translators should have used Jesus' name rather than Christ. There is only one Greek word in the Bible that the translators translated as "Christ," and it is Christos (khirs-tos'), meaning anointed. Mr. Strongs and others who published interlinear's added, "Messiah, an epithet of Jesus." If we use the rule of first mention, the first place the King James version uses the word "anointed" is in the area where David had a horn oil poured out over his head. The term was supposed to be translated as "consecrated," rather than "anointed." To be consecrated implies the person has seen something. In Jesus' case, he saw what Father did and heard what Father said – he was consecrated by staying in CONTACT with Father.

The Greek word the translators should have used is the root word, chrio (khree'o), meaning through the idea of contact, and then Mr. Strongs and the others added: "to smear or rub with oil." A different root word is chraomia (khrah'-om-ahee), which means to be able to handle and furnish what is needed. What we think we need was supplied from the foundation, and whatever is required for spiritual or physical life will flow out of or to you as you make contact with your Source Father. Another awesome root word is cheir (khire), meaning "congener," meaning a person of the same kind of category or class. So, what do we discover when we contact Father our Divine Mind? We find out we are in the same category or class as Father. One more root word is cheimon (khi-mone'), meaning the idea of a channel, as in pouring rain, or may I say, we become a channel of the Living Water (Word) of Father, to flood out of our being, like torrents of Living Water.

So, now you know why I prefer to use the word contact with our Divine Mind (Source – Father), rather than Christ as in you, as the thought that Christ is Jesus in you. Jesus did not want to stay mankind's source; he wanted mankind to Connect or Contact Father as their only Source.

So, it is better to understand that Contact with Father in you is your hope of showing forth (glory) who you are.

**Faith – Peter – the center of the head, pineal gland.**

Peter is our first Apostle. Peter symbolizes faith in the power of Holy Breath (Spirit), which was accelerated in him by watching Jesus' ministry with the people, his character, and nature; the faith capacity when staying in contact with the Divine Mind. His main acceleration event was when Jesus appeared to him after resurrecting himself and did not condemn him for denying Jesus. The Voice of One, influencing our thought, dramatically affects our body and its facilities. If a part of our consciousness has not been accelerated or quickened in harmony with our Divine Mind, then there is a paralysis in our facilities. When the Voice of One is freely flowing to one's thoughts, then the inner systems of our body are energized to the point that every cell is a generation, and all forms of inactivity disappear. Spiritual thought and real thinking come forth.

## Thought

Some thoughts come from Father - our Source-Papa, and then there are thoughts that come from being anxious.

There are seven references to Jesus telling the people to "take no thought." He said, "Take no thought for your life, what you shall eat or drink, nor for your body, what you shall put on, for tomorrow, and how you will speak when required to (Spirit speaks in you and through you).

Seven times, Jesus said, "Take no thought." Seven is the biblical number for perfection, spiritual maturity, and divine intervention. The phrase "take thought," as it is written in Greek, is merimano (mer-im-hah'-o), and it means "to be anxious." A further meaning is not to be anxious by distractions.

Take no thought – do not be anxious for your life or this world.

Jesus instructed the people and all who would hear his words in the future to return to putting our lives in the faith of his and our Source-Papa. The first race of humanity (A'dam) left their constant contact with the

Voice of their Source-Papa. They began to be anxious about their lives and state of being, which produced the distractions of carnality and religiosity. Once they believed the lie of separation from Father, they saw it in themselves and said, "We are naked." Then they became more anxious and sought to hide from their Source-Papa with fig leaves, symbolizing the clothing of religiosity.

**Our Rhythm of Life** remains constant no matter what else is happening. It is not subject to the opinions or beliefs of mankind, no matter how changeable and unsubstantial they are. It is constant, perpetual, eternal, and immutable (unchangeable). Spirit responds only to its own intelligent order. In addition, wherever your Holy Spirit is allowed to effortlessly flow, life and beauty, perfection and goodness, and absolute order prevail. Yes, the realization of this Life does bring experience, but whether we ever realize its presence or not, we are still Father's most glorious Vessel.

It is a rare person that spends any quality time in silence. The world is built around satisfying the senses with sensual pleasures and influences. In fact, very few there are who can actually silence their thoughts. And yet, Scripture exhorts us, "To be still and know." One of the English words, "Still," comes from the Hebrew word "chashah (khaw-shaw'), meaning to hush and keep silent.

Psalm 4:4 gives instruction, "To stand in awe, and quit living with a mistaken identity syndrome (sin): stay in contact with Father while you rest; hush and be quiet – listen to Father's voice of love." Psalm 45:10 says, "Hush and be quiet, and intimately know that I Exist as your Father: I Exist in all people of the earth, and I Exist in all the earth." Psalm 84:4, "Happy and well off are they who comfortably EXIST as my Holy Temple: they in quietness and silence reveal My nature in them." RERichmond Tree of Life Bible

In Mark 4:39, we find that Jesus was asleep in a boat with his disciples, and to them a great storm was raging, and they ran to get Jesus, saying do you not care if we perish? He got up and went to the front of the boat, forbade the harsh wind, and said to the storm, Perfection from you, hush and be quiet." The clouds and rain returned to their intention– gently watering the earth.

The disciples were afraid, even when Jesus was in their boat with them.

Guess who is in your boat? The Father of all Creation, hush and be quiet - and speak perfection and peace over your world softly.

If you live with a "sense of lack," your Father God might not be your Shepherd in reality and experience. Selah

Psalm 23 - The Lord is my Shepherd; I Exist not wanting...

# Bibliography

The Voice of my Holy Breath / Spirit, drawing out of me and explaining what I have learned over the past 36 years, as of 2021, and Spirit speaking understanding that cannot be learned by a surface level or carnal understanding of the written word.

Strong's Numbers and Concordance with Expanded Greek-Hebrew Dictionary. Copyright (c) 1994, Biblesoft and International Bible Translators, Inc.

Many Ancient Spiritual-Biblical Dictionary's

RERichmond Tree of Life Bible Translations

E-Sword Bible Program – Greek and Hebrew

Many Ancient Mystic (Spiritual seekers) Books.

To Contact Dr. Roy E. Richmond: 405-204-0713
drroyerichmond@cox.net Social Media:
Facebook Roy E. Richmond | YouTube Dr. Roy E. Richmond
For more books and other study material:
https://www.lulu.com/spotlight/royrichmond

www.drroyerichmond.com

Copyright 2023 RERichmond

Published by RERichmond Publishing

625 SW 158th Terrace | Oklahoma City, Ok 73170

*"Providing Portions to Them from whom Nothing is Prepared"*
*Nehemiah 8:10*

Printed in April 2023
by Rotomail Italia S.p.A., Vignate (MI) - Italy